Tenebrous Yearning

Poetry of T. F. Lanning

Tenebrous Yearning

Copyright © 2011 by T. F. Lanning

Library of Congress Control Number: 2012904260

ISBN: 978-0-9853135-1-7

Printed in the U.S.A.

Tenebrous Yearning is a variety of poetry written over several years in chronological order, exploring much inspiration throughout my life; a great collection which grew with me. Finding solace, exploring love, and unrequited love, yearning, dreams, cryptic poems, fantasy, longing, wisdom, truth, darkness, poignant reverie, and more. I treasure these poems as if they were my own children, and they are. And at last, after 17 long years, they can finally be shared with the world.

To my Mother, for being there with insight, and to her family.

To my Father, for his tenacity and perseverance.

To my Father's Brother, Lee (Ozzy), my Dad misses you.

And for my mentor Osiris, for teaching and guiding the way.

My email is khepharos@gmail.com

Contents

I began writing these poems when I was just 15 years old, in the year 1995 - at a beautiful place I'll never forget in Calabasas, California. It was a scene lush with trees, flowers, and a slope where below a stream ran through under a bridge. People used to get married by a gazebo far off in the distance along the watery ravine, and for me it was where I unlocked my ability to write. While partners made their vows to each other, I unknowingly made a promise to inspiration, and a yearning to find myself in writing. I'm sure you'll find something in these pages I poured my soul into over the long years past perhaps inspiring, poignant, heartfelt, or touching to you.

Bright Foliage   5/29/95

Trees, leaves, pollinating bees. A monarch flies high, but where will
it go? Travel with the flow of the wind, maybe so. Flies pick the
heck out of me. I guess I'll climb a tree, where the squirrels roam
free.

Pluck a petal from its crest, and raid a sparrow's nest. Look at the
butterfly! How it gently hitches a ride on a breeze. I run after it,
hoping to catch it, but I trip over me.

As I sit for mile-long hours under a magical fable, I'm locked within
its power – the beautiful tippity-top of a maple cradle. I eavesdrop
on tumbling leaves; they spin like acrobats, whirling and landing on
my knees.

Tickle-tickle the grass itches so! I peer up and leer at the song of a
crow's peaceful cheer. I can hear the droplets tingling down in the
water bog, traveling far with a river making a raft ride of infinite
trickle.

Dead bark hangs down, avoiding the hell of wind, eroding their
spirits and breaking once awesome green. Their glory is gone, and
we live on to see another bright day.

Do we break as easy as a branch? Perhaps we live as long as a tree,
with roots for feet and limbs with leaves. We sprout and die,
leaving inner soul, and venturing out into the unknown. To the
Pharaohs of Egypt, or to the Gardens of Greece, where shall we go?

So I start a poem anew, sixteen already and things seem blue. I don't know who you are, but the feeling I have for you is quite new. Very lonely now, you're so far away from me – but when my heart yawns, it calls for thee. Who are you? What do you need from me? Your love, it stands as a beautiful shady tree. You may never know the face that is behind the shadow, nor what desire in flames may be. A gap that needs to be filled by you – could it be? In a shroud of mystery I can only hide from you, and this is the only clue. Don't worry I'll just follow you wherever you may be. Someday this time of our youth like the sands of an hourglass will pass. It's sad... as for me, never to be a boy again – a man. Love, it is a splendid power indeed.

Hard to Say

2/8/97

I thought I'd write a poem just so you'd knew I have this special feeling for you. I don't know what to say. So many feelings get in the way. What kind of poem is this? Don't throw it away! Just another rhyme comin' from my head, that's all okay?! I really need to tell you what I mean by all this dreaming bliss; maybe I could seal my love with a kiss? Sorry to bug you all the time this way – forget it! I lost my mind back there along the way...

Yearning Past

2/16/97

Time keeps flashing by. Every second, every moment, fate is always standing by. Remembering when I was a kid. It was so sweet and enchanted, where hopes and dreams were so real, and life's realities were abandoned. Living each day without fearing the next, mirrors throwing images never worried how they would reflect back.

Sea Shelter

2/20/97

My love, you are the sweetest droplet that ripples through my heart. Waves that come crashing down, washing away the struggle I feel when we part. You rip through my soul and purge the thirst of lust. This love is of an enchanted kind, though I fear these waves have buried it and become a treasure all in rust.

A noble love so grand was felt some time ago. Sword resting, gripped in my torn hands. Through muddy flats and dense forest gapping over riverbanks, flowing eternal peace in this life, not the fight against the knight's lance. Wishing all in my heart I could have loved her; I wasn't there. I needed more charm in the dancing fate I dreamed in romance. Just a frame of time I needed; a bright flare in life's devilish marching advance. Of skin tight on tender muscle, a heart-sinking glance. A love so sweet, tears would erupt, waking spirits at the sight of her face. I wanted nothing more than a complete royal love with her; as a blacksmith pounding with anvil and hammer, constructing a beautiful full suit of armor. With loyal honor we could have forged a love so strong, never to be broken by the clubbing mace or another knight's code of honor. Possessionless I gallop along now. Without a castle, my fair maiden, or my word I wanted to promise her. Swing with the axe, down with the branches. The sparkling water that falls between us shall be everlasting. Farewell my lost love. I cower as my hands tremble in fear. My sword is gone, and power has left me. Oh! Take my hand, I am so lonely. Let me rest in death; my fair lady, thee.

Futile Seed   3/3/97

Now I dwindle slowly and fall away, not feeling the full effect of
each new day. Death awaiting at every stepping thought, any
feeling of pain. The vast fields of color and plenty shall be harvest
at the last rain, but my heart and soul plants seeds of rot never to
be cleansed of its stain, only to die and wither away. The sky holds
a dark hover as my heart is constantly in battle with toil and vain.
To conquer inner thought is to destroy any outside reign. It
appears now, as the clouds part and the sharp thorns prick, the
deep scarlet drip shall be fruitful in ridding myself of poor
squander and love's acid rain.

High-rise hotels with overflowing coin pails. Losers and winners made out of thin air. Taxi armadas racing by, fares and wages getting high. Skating down the street, skating down on hard concrete, blacktop burning up like a stovetop. Sun scorching my ass, trying to get shade and relax. Like an oasis hidden in sand, a carless parking lot really hits the spot as my thirst is quenched because of a really awesome skating lot. My heart is speeding as I grind into smooth rock. All of the sudden my heart stops as a security cop strides into view. Badge shining and a dumb golfing car to ride in, he tells me to get off onto the sidewalk as I flip him off. Looking for another spot, trying not to get caught. Flashing lightning slashes through bright light, sky turning into desert night. Drops of rain appear on grip tape. Fearing the rust on my bearings, I rush home to listen to some rockin' Green Day!

Shira, I lost so much sleep last night, writing this poem by a dim light. I thought as the hours passed by, what it is inside my soul that turns me to shy. Besides the fact that I know I'll use a thousand papers to form my style of a love rhyme. And I felt a sudden fear or dread; wanting to embrace the soul-spirit within you – a power that could tell no lies, like a feather floating, drifting in the sky. But my cramped heart was all wound up. All full of lusts, a filthy mind. I was held back, confused. But I always knew that if I didn't keep your interest – a poem, a touch, a sigh, your love might drain away and you would leave, filling another heart with this loving state of mind. So I sit with stringy hair in my hand, playing a guitar tune way past nine. With all these undying strums that ricochet off heart strings blasting out of an amp, a wall plastered with mattresses. Tones leaping out, a feeling I wish could melt your soul with mine. I know this sounds awesome, and it stains me and I can't tell why. How many poems will it be for those without an answer, past sorrow for lovers to be, only left behind. Please don't stick it on your wall. Don't laugh at it, or hold regret. If the soul fits wear it. I want you to be the only clothes in my closet that fit me right I swear it. And I feel like da' bomb king after that neat last sentence. And you, beautiful queen Shira, I want to play a solo for you first before I undress you. I'm sorry I had to turn such a heart-sinking poem into a trashy heap. But to tell you the truth I'm in this love. In heat!! One of thy best poems I've writ, Shira sweet!

Alone   5/10/97

Am I alone in this world? There isn't any infrastructure – any
other's mind to look inside of to try to find. And the brain, with
waves as complex as intricacies in tall rocky mountain caves, where
feelings are felt, and the mysteries of life are puzzles in an infinite
maze. Judgemental we are of those along with us in this wild
parade. We waste our time worrying about others marching and
falling, putting skin and sight together to form a sculpture of
human character in which we ourselves are made.

Irrational Eye   5/11/97

I saw the only girl I loved. I glanced at her from afar, feeling a
mysterious air enshroud me as I eyed her golden hair flowing
down. What fantasies I have I long to see. She stood, and I wept a
turmoil within. I'd never say what needed to be said. To find those
rusted feelings chained and locked inside. It was barbaric, as I fell
on my own soul. I was a body on an axe pendulum, with a deep red
rose in one hand. The gore and sickly hold it had – yet it sparked a
passionate love fire my waiting heart desired; I needed to have. My
depths were burning. Nothing in the universe could save me. I
never knew love's cruel hands could touch me like this. She goes far
away to where I do not know, and to this day never have I known
such fate as unrequited bliss.

Hollow Mind

Living in our own worlds within the mind, alone inside. Some you meet find fault with anything they can find and tear down your sense of pride. There is no freedom from the chain in which we are locked in: our total soul combined. Living life to the fullest is the greatest mystery. We are all constantly seeking those with the same feelings as our own and have our comforting. And the evils become apparent when you recognize others' desire, greed, and envy. Everything's a state of mind in the world's empty.

Sad Soliloquy

5/17/97

Her vase is dry, the flowers are gone. The rainy clouds are covering the sun. Itch a scratch and wonder what happened to the goddess of love. There is no inspiration. She was the only one. Feeling coming to a dead end. Blood-letting rhymes draining me, to hell my aura shall be sent.

Burning

6/1/97

It burns me up inside. It stings the heart and buries my emotion deep, axing down the branches of love, each fruit wrapping a seed. In the mud they fall, rotting away, feeling never grown, just post-mortem decay. Into hollow trees, suffering they grow, sprouting demon's heads that shrivel to die. Ripping me up, screaming and clawing inside. They prey on this dark heart and pry my soul open, spreading bloodless lies when my heart is already stolen.

Jagged sharp glass bends the light shining through darkness; problems in my mind becoming killing madness. Spiked swinging chains surround me, a nerve swells with anxiety. My skin wall I leap out of, my soul searching for a place to shout from. Love is oblivious in the mind that wants to shine straight through stained glass shattered by dead pieces of time. It's rare to find antique memories. I sold them all for a sour lime.

Lost   6/11/97

Feeling pain right and left, I keep on holding onto regret. Nothing stays in place. The cement always stays wet. Poetry is the one that lets me dwell in my mind, to communicate to a cloaked shadow, and have comfort in its pure clear watered shrine. Perhaps it is the one that winds my pace and follows every rhythm on my neurotic spiked platform which I crawl upon. My empty soul drips green blood. I'm not a leprechaun. I stare at the sun, stinging my eyes. Where is the gold? Is the rainbow full of lies?

Freed   6/17/97

I'll find a place of splendor if I follow this magical road, knowing
this path will take me wherever I want to go. Every key on my
ring's a skull. A million mountains I must scale. Lost love is a coin
pitched into a foggy well. No wishes are thought for, as my heart
heals strong. Mending is the stitcher that has overcome hell, and it
tears up a nightmare I've lived for so long.

Fear   6/30/97

Hell is the tool I use, and heaven is a rope where I hang. Flesh is my
hiding place. Your soul is mine to waste. Blood-shot eyes don't tell
the truth when a man's eyes don't move. Scared straight out of your
skin, bones rotting without your blood filled veins.

Today   7/6/97

So many paths I can take. From here, the fork that splits life is up
ahead. Canyons to be crossed; bad signs to help me get lost in wind,
crooked roads leading to sketched paintings of portraits on a dead-
end road behind, ahead. Bridges span over each highway I take,
patching over fears I create. Others pass, but I give no right away.
On my own this road is bumpy. Time will tell the story right, if I'm
lucky. Can't let sun in, for it won't be beautiful today. I have to
watch the road and run over emotions that get in my way. Is there a
detour behind the fog? A straight overpass to let me overcome a
bad rear view mirror, to make it for me up ahead clearer? This life
has to be wild on one of these confusing one-way roads. No more
doubts about where I'm going to go. I'll exit off at that next
beautiful scenic way where my emotions and imaginations don't
stop going away. A place of strong hopes and fed desires, never
starved like an island cast away. Millions of adventures lived in my
view that conquered the day. And on this quick road I find I get
older, and bottle all my precious thoughts and feelings, breathe in,
and hold on to the future. Today.

Starting Barricade

I don't need this gloomy leech that sucks off my life force and eats my null brain, turning inner society into a lost, confused minds bane. All those on the outside will never know the intricacy of terror that I have I don't show. Happy faces drown me. Polka-dot monkeys of cotton I tear up and they fill me when an evil anxiety. A blank room full of figments of imagination where creativity is nothing when there is no door knocking. If the bell is rung, it's a stranger. When I hear knocking, I know it's my friend. The door is never opened, nor is it locked. When they say nothing to get in, I twist the knob. Nobody has a key to unlocked barricaded doors that I'm behind. I don't hide from a creature that has enough substance for me to dwell inside.

Black Quarry

7/15/97

Its only comfort when it's rotten outside, gives me inspiration in the things I write. The color black is my shining light. My domain of darkness is the cave of life. It'll be sadder today, I know I'm right.

Time's Extol   7/29/97

Pre-Poem -

Time. It is a gigapolis for me, or a mouse hole of darkness which I'm
crammed into; the creator and destroyer. The bomb that ticks your
last seconds and it doesn't need a fuse. It's nature's way of having
organization. There is no evident plan. Its fate, if you want to call it
by its name. Space would be void without time, and time must keep
track of space. We are inseparable from the clock's hands as they
wave in their motions, spins, and our many moods - an hourglass
lacking sand in a future of tall panes of colorful crystal glass.

Poem -

It sneaks by in an invisible shadow we enshroud it as. The day is
done, sun going down. Sleep in our castle minds and wake with
sunrise. The day is all we have. Our habits are encrusted next in
line. Keeping thoughts and memories alive, filling our incomplete
limited time. Do not fear your deaths, but fear pain; let our mind's
god do the rest of the calculating. In true life, our hell is locked
within the mind. We banish ourselves and with similes of emotions,
heaven or hell be the rhyme. Just when justice should win, we can
all be the victims of an evil crime. Some on earth cut their own head
off to avoid their predestined sign. Nature of sky, or hole to flames;
you define where it is that you'll lie in either of these brain plaguing
whims. Time is not short, nor is it forever. If we weren't born we
needn't surrender. Live your life. Savor until the last shiver; when
we're all just revealed as a headstone at a funeral in November.

Sentry   8/6/97

I diligently and constantly am trying to find words for my random
emotions I must define. If only I wasn't held up by innocent, spying
whispers which has my soul occupied. I will find within myself
what it is I need to be complete. To always be attacking with
questions, to imprison with my mental guards; they cannot escape.
The mind is a slave, and its captor residing inside itself. Dwelling at
times in its own torment of the master's floggings dealt. The body
being a machine, and the mind is a grand ivory column on a view
from what is felt.

My life is but a piece of shattered glass on earth's massive glass pane. The view can be spectacular, but limited by dreams. I can only work, hide in my space, hope, and let time run away. I think as one to myself, it isn't life, but my words that huddle before the attack and ambush my emotions. The naked faeries; in defense they lack. You cannot win any fight, only your own. The battle is won only until within yourself you see it conquered alone. I must say before I am zero, we will be joined until the end. Our consciousness is simply an extended dream; on our machine does it depend.

We only have a day contrasting to the world's past. Humans we call ourselves, dinosaurs that are extinct sooner than midnight, the clock hand does pass. The earth will live until the sun is rind, and space as it is, continues to peel and divide, to constantly multiply. I see how frail we all are on our mental seesaw. Even the strongest and fit of men and mind had weaknesses embedded within. Our skin is but a wrapper on our god's ingenious in which we are forced to live. Perception is limited to what is, and if our minds tell it true, we simply are not fallen from any religion, but followers of a gene of beliefs passed on like any hopeless giving virtue; it can be a sin.

It helps to pity those who just don't know. If you're above the rest within, it's substance that can't be spilled, it can never show. You will ultimately be thrown in your grave by other likenesses in skin, but deadly in ways of thought and foolish personal goals that seek to be satisfied by your rot on their whim. We must see ourselves in new light of ways never before seen. And to learn life is comfort and approximating.

Words are simply plain compared to the mind that feels what's hiding behind them. If the wish is to be secure and seek to confide in yourself, show not personal emotions. You must let them dwell. Fleeting to the outside subjects them to other beings' relentless inner hell, escaping their bars with like feelings that cannot be kept in their cells. The warden has posted universal bail. Killers, rapists, thieves, the mentally insane; all are freed without justice and undeserved liberty, roaming to do their uncontrolled labors. Each has a purpose, an engraved name. Feelings destroyed Rome in a thousand universes. Our mind's god forced non-believers to burn millions. Destiny should not be followed, but created to serve the host – the unified spirit that one deserves the most. We are all animals like it or not, born an unknowing evil, brought up in hope to be good. Some did not receive love needed as a young child should. Everyone is burning in a flame deciding, or worrying about another poor soul's angst. It's sickening to see what pirates we are to walk these foolish planks. The gold is where we see it. The eye is not always trained; to uncover what we want out of life, we must dig at the right vein.

Life always goes on. Don't worry about how it will end. Handle yourself with control, you can then do anything. Our mind is our brain's tool; a vast secret safe. Not a carat nor jewel, but a billion chemical reactions, and the combo must be in the right place. The storage combines all that we own, rich or poor. I know that intellect is the rich man's sharpest sword. Sometimes I feel mixed with so many eager, anxious entities that creep around in my mind. I tell myself, Travis, you still have time. Everyone is alone in the ways of their mind. I seek its shelter against all others slinging poison pieces of mind at my eardrums, assailing my neurons inside. Deadly as a Minotaur's hooves, they unleash beliefs as they wish to gain useless surrender on your mind's shell, they constantly dig. Everyone has a purpose to your life, along with suiting the limits of their own. Ask not of one anything that doesn't know their reasons beyond thoughts untold.

We are merely here to serve the matter undefined by the human eye. To have reason and a cognitive mind, the real truths we should seek to answer are the ones we need to obey in our own lives. It's taken billions of years for any group of atoms to reason by looking out on the fields and sky, how and why the flowers die. The world is ours to learn in our time. And our inner emotions flash by, enabling us to hold on, or let go of this life. Some distraught turn to genocide, some decide their only answer is suicide. But the concrete answer is found in the mind; it must be deciphered, and it asked why. The blatant reply is simply unfolded again, and a paradox is met. The truth to me is the one that is lived by. A program and path in space and time, the will to make my own decisions, and live a simple, thoughtful life is my true bible; my master god until I die.

As the sky rumbles, I urge myself to create a dark side of me to live within, on the outside without. Passion is stronger used with no outside force. Objects that hurt me, and then it's comprehended all wrong. No book's page can be torn from this binding with a title given and no consent. What writer would misprint my first chapters, and mean no harm? For it was their crooked pen, their dealings clearly in ink, marked all wrong. I must develop false love for an unfinished book. Truthfully, my life's pages must be updated. The ink has not dried. I see spots of space that need to be filled with new color of life. Enjoying aged antiques without shine, now that I'm finding all my buried treasures? I once was a pirate as a child. It's recent that I'm able to dig up why I buried my sense of gold in an empty hole. I hid from society. An entity, make shift shelter where I stored my ultimate personal emotions. I had no other. And through rain and rot, I've at long last discovered poetry is the tool I use to uncover my dark past. A comfort on a web spun pure from reason, and an arachnid's legs vibrating the silk strands, chilling my mortal spine. It's insight as to how I dwell in the variable depths of the shadowed mind. And now magnified in this light, my thunder I hear in the clouds at night is the fear or sorrows past, and it triggers me to think of a blankness lived my whole life. I'm but a poet to fog my own mind.

I loved her in the world known to none. My emotions stomp me. I wanted to kiss her and feel the sun. My life is yearning for her love, but feeling embarrassed and locked up inside; conveying a hiding not even unto her I can confide. I wish I could love her, to kiss her tender hand. You are a petite rose; feeling my heart turning to sand, grains falling, slipping through my hands. I fear I fear love, for you overcome mine for thee. It would be somber sweet to cherish you instead of a poem. This is the only way I can see, that my heart to give is too sewn up from my love constantly writing. Love is your need. It is mine, my story. People hurt, I must let you know. If I lose myself in your waves, I will be wanting to love always, ending in an overflow; and the water still pours slow. My heart's rhythm is speeding fast. The only way to love is to accept the fact. Your skull holds orbs of beauty. Your hair is sleek, moody. I see your beauty through the soul, but nevertheless, it's what the eye beholds. I'm merely hiding behind the mask, poetry is the sum. Fantasy points her finger at me. I want to show you love; next will too many times be an if, and, or but. Something I must discover – the sun of times past. I search hopelessly for what color it is... does it lack? Your aura is the one picture that touches life. Oh, is it love? Let me weep in song, for I tell you my feelings. I always was misplaced in trivial love.

The Voyage Alone 2/11/98

My love flew away, I need to say. Give me wings so I may fly too, to find my one love so true. Over sea and desert sand, could she be far off in some distant land? The seas I sail show no signs of her, and mortal as I am, my heart bleeds in awe, knowing my voyage can only last so long. Her beauty turning my insides to quicksand, a fading glimpse into the spyglass at youth lost without. When will I find across the seas of life, past seagulls astray, a breeze of salt spray upon a shore where both of us find peace with calm words and love between - to anchor my heart in this deep dream. My tattered sails have need of rest from such dire winds. To explore these endless waters alone sinks hopes and all my treasures of soul. A bounty lost on the waves where I once traveled treacherous miles to find this fleeting and vanishing love.

Trap 2/24/98

The axe falls with desert light. Crowds slither like serpents to see such a horrible sight. With torrents of rain to pour from clouds, scarlet flows silent under dark shrouds. The sun is gone, and a black sky over doom passes overhead. The elevated axe starts its grinding fall again. Marching forward, these punished souls deservedly fall. Past the bladed platform, paradise is vanquished for them all. Perhaps they'll fall in love with killers and be kissed the same way. Or roam the earth, dying over again, becoming the plague. When they find some peace in a soul's life, they're cut away to serve another, banished to follow the tides of time; some becoming faith devotees and evils searching out pleasure. The end is the only escape. Life is a maze, you are trapped in it. That soul is inside you, it cannot be erased.

Dream   3/10/98

I saw her sweet face in a glance. Never again would my eyes dance
as they did in that captivating trance. With a myriad of shells
strewn down the shore, her eyes drift along the painted horizon to
meet mine; as beautiful as a thousand tides, each becoming more
elegant over time. Beauty's shell never breaks with age if emotion
we bury is deep in sand beneath the waves. Softly touching lips
against mine – our soul between us shall not divide. Crashing
waves drown and quiet my melodious heart. Tides carrying us
away, and saddened when we part. The sand is sifted and I take the
shell in hand. The image fades into the breeze, now small in the
distance, disappearing at the end of vision, sinking into the sea. The
shell I keep and will always wait for thee.

Ode to Poor Fuzzy   3/13/98

A squirrel lies flat on a road, wheels speeding off, chased by its
guilt. The pity is in the heart, man or stone, when a living creature's
bell tolls. The soul is in the body, yet it must decay. It's killed in one
place never to come back from the other again. The body rests, and
the soul withers away. The squirrel is spread upon the ground,
with an unzipped outside, and insides all around. A last silence is
felt, and time stops as a final heartbeat is sound to the land of tall
trees and acorns.

Fated   3/17/98

Nothing houses a soul. After tears and faith what remains is blood
and bone. So omnipresent is fate to life. Only cloaked daydreams
reveal the future from inside. Reflections of a faded past, in one's
advancing destiny, find a chance at last. A sixth sense existing in the
body, trapped in a knowledge knowing fate. It speaks of what is to
happen before you know it's too late as an omen - if you lose it, it is
haze.

Endless Always   3/25/98

When I look to find what is inside, tears forge within, with rain
from the sky. Tomorrow will be beautiful. So closer will I be to the
world, intimate and free. If the sun is a shadows glow, its shine
reveals a deep passion and pleasure to remember her sweet eyes in
love. Fate is known before time is memory. Where is an answer,
where is my true love? Might she be a soul as me, with nothing but
memories of our time without one another? The sun is but a
shadow. Where is fate, but in tomorrow. Your eyes glisten inside
and share a tear I cannot hide. Always, my heart will love you
forever inside.

I escape my chamber as a shade down the dark shaft, close to stone walls. Traps set for the living ensnared by the dead, as the entity changes to fog, delivered from the sealed grave. Breath is given, a body taken; the searching soul is made human. Heat, dust, and scorching sand with sun to mold flesh and wind to dry bones, a spirit is joined and life takes this hand. Ancients buried this rotting rejoiced corpse, desiring to resurrect blood and bones - a man.

The ground is naked, bodies strewn far and few are seen, mostly dead ashes wet with fallout rain. The final hell is at last outside the brain. Darkness fell on that sadistic eve. The apocalypse swept as human evil reigned. Chaos came with battle of God against Satan's slaves, and in conflict the world tremored heavily, engulfed in crematory flames. From the heavens God saw what the demons had done, and by thunder and hurricane he drenched the fiery storm, clearing smoke to uncover the sun. A wicked fight ensued; acid and claws to shred fists and skin. The inferno raged, melting multitudes of men. God did nothing to save a world long before enveloped in murderous sin. Souls dragged to hell faced eternal wrath of Satan's kin. The blood soaked atmosphere fogged sight in searing red. The séance writhed with screams of terror and repentance, and priests read aloud holy testament. Pogrom as it was, everything alive was slain, either taken to hell as slave, or faded into the hate of a shade. Burn and boil exploded the terrestrial canopy. Life existed only in millions of scorched dictionaries. God was last of immortal vigor, transforming into one last human. The cannibal demons had been sealed from the earthly hell and up rose Satan to obliterate time and space once and for all. The macabre image walked through the bounteous flames and met with the final blood rushing alive, and horribly cut off its life. The universe twisted violently, for matter or mind, good and evil, and time and space were destroyed utterly. And so, nothing only breathed of the fiery tomb which was man.

It's closed up space all around, feeling trapped in liquids bubbling.
It's quiet as I'm pumped in canals going up and down. The flow
leads me to palpitations. It must be anger within a creature's heart
that makes it throb so soundly, so loud. Outside sensations beat
down the crowds, and clears barriers of dead inflammations locked
in their cells. Battles come to halt amidst the dark cage, and heavy
breathing must create dense fogs in rage. Inside a hollow column
the crowds risk fear, as transport is interrupted by cries and panic,
and unearthed dispossession is near. Thrown from the falling
tower, and nothing to mend a broken, crushed, bloody flower. Flesh
is opened in coldness after the crimson-stained murder. Silent and
still, the crowds have no escape to steal as a blade inserts itself into
an army hasting to entail reports to one master that cannot feel.
Cold and rushing, edged metal chops away thin slivers of decay.
Horror arises, and riot it would be, if the massacred governor were
still alive, running. The crowds are ripped apart, and hell in its
zenith is a dismembering masochist's art. The crowds die, finite in
count, spewed from sore body wounds, they are exiled to rest on
maggot breeding ground. Only does the terror claim, a skull
severed from its mount. Dead we are, evaporating crowds, and a
killer freed from his bout.

And you, who would you rather have survive? The earth herself, or a mortal lacking the earth destined to die. She who was born first, of lifeless entity shall outlive all, amidst man's conscious calamity. In Gaia lies Uranos, and in the sky lies mother earth. Only in existence do simple actions of desires give way to birth. Chaos began the joy and turmoil, and so it shall end. Man walks upon the earth in spite of man. Ye that harvests disaster, yields crops to tend. We are god; death is the only other. Believe in yourself. Not the imaginations of another.

Oh, lone tree that does hang above over me, your branches manifold, sway gently bent stitched amongst a beautiful green canopy. Trunk surrounded by a jungle of cement. Birds sing within to converse, to remind foliage to grow anew, that leaves may be drenched by the new rain. An aged sacred celestial seed, there you remain a spectacle to open eyes. The zephyr currents under your shade flow up your height. A perched crow, the darting butterfly, a sitting youth. While we pine away as this tree, in no such time shall it know its beauty, but only to horizons of eyes built to find an experience. Searching an earth of one kind, with no possible other realities in space. Thrust upon aging conscious ways until sorrowful impermanence finds our husk barren in the winds, when nothing can only remember our hearts that once beat.

My appearance morphs without my consent. Time owns it, a mirror of black. Dashing into what I see, perhaps to shatter time and space, time the teller of destiny. Hold my spear of memories Mnemosyne, as I relive myself again, when life was in spirited full bloom; roses thornless and trails long. A vaulted poignant sky and sweet shelter under her trees, living, seeing faintly in the water that reflects all life, flowing gently; an image as nebulous as god within me. The spear of time cuts forth, leaving and forgetting a jagged rusty pole, with its blade, a golden edge. The advancing brink of existence, all lucid and gleam, with a sharp pointed head. A javelin of time, piercing forward, thrown by what was living tomorrow. An end of the momentous journey is but a slight quivering, and soon vanquished memory. Time regains its steady path. But life lives not according to another's aim. Live to the moment and time has purpose. Love the just and hate what you must, but live not in chapters closed, in dust.

Eros' arrow pierced me, and a sweet potion was sent by Circe. The sight of you sends quivers through my body. Love's arrow hits its target sharply, and the potion turns to poison. The only antidote found is by sipping of your love and admiring your warm crystal fountain, a statuette hand carved as it seems, shining and sparkling in melodious proportion. For love to be, six senses must adjoin to feel like one. I bestow these on thee, and set my emotions free in your green fields of sun by the sea. The sound of your pitches fall gently, eloquently to my ears, like dew drops of voice tingling on petals that are your fingers, mixed by love's harmonious pollen of rejoice. The sixth sense lies in you, violet flower, purple, or blue. It is the emotion that plays its lyre, and hinders me from finding the true fire. Searching my soul I find only you, and fantasies yearning to be free too. Life, no matter where you are, nor where you go, I now know that without any love, my tender beauty, is but empty. If obstruction does fill your heart, let me pour my sand of love in your hands; open them apart and fill them ardently. If this time we must pass, sorrowfully. I'll whisper my loving so that you may hear, for in the waves my love, you've swept me away. Yet for you, still I am but the wind; invisible, while you ponder who it is, who it has been. As long as the wind breathes, and the earth brings fires like love, I'll look through the flames and see you, shining like my crystal star up above.

The unfinished rose...

Let me leave this place, oh tangled chains, for you keep me with no reason but that I am without native soil or of a proper season. My wits need stretching, I admit. So then give me books as company, and a sweetness for the salt sea on my tongue, a safe voyage as I near an island home. With an iron hull to pass through exotic coral, to moor the stern on a faraway isle. Only blithe beasts and one content man on this land do roam. Build a structure to keep out the cold, and call it home. Store necessities within, fortify it to guard the soul. Only a peaceful long life could come of all this. My young veins yearn to travel to the archipelago scattered out like broken skeletal wrists. The palms sway in their infinite breeze, and I hear them calling. In the shallow clear water do I stand amongst starfish and sand. Our tryst is void until I find a way to break these scorned chains, and sail far to a beautiful unmapped distant land.

Muse, the sound of words find each other, you make love to words I join together. Emotions sew rows of tone, from seeds sprouting long in either thorn ridden branches not crested by any rose, or loving ivy always trimmed sadly, and hating it when it grows. You fervent words torment in silent eloquence, as a puppet bard yearns for true love in repentance. A poignant shiver of rites ends the eternal flow where the searching poet is happily lost in the hall of inspirative tone. Imbued reverence to the torches lit and passed. Truth is cloaked by Apollo's lyre, and a colorful array of words amassed. If real passion exists, flames glow bright in the grand hall. Life without passion fades things to death, and grades one contradictory test for all.

Is there a shade of sweet tenderness in thee? Beneath the bark enclosing your soft breasts, and your heart as my staple of divinity, ripples what emotion if any, within its vicinity? The color of leaves live with the sun in unity, existing in a bond with warm light, its love. The tree's naked cover, shedding and unvisited by the dove, unable to see and feel in the cold, the true love of spring that was once alive one hundredfold. Roots buried that were once planted with love I water still, and the soil drinks my soul, a dusty requiem of a crow. But when the leaves change their colors with the autumn of love, bright red and orange like a patch of ripe pumpkins ready to be carved - to exile ones like the dove, the wind echoes through our valley; the leaves dying and falling on Mother Earth's body. Shade I loved I pine away in. You shed your deceitful love and I shed tears to water soil in the branches above. Then spring arrives again; flowers sweep fields, melting golden love in man. I'll find what shade I can on your stump, that once above was the leafy shade of your sweet tenderness where we first made love.

Our story is the second Juliet and Romeo. My heart is poisoned, afflicted with pain of love. Your blood runs out of a warm wound with you dispatching yourself in spite of facing my love, or that your love lacks full bloom. We die together, but we live on as Clotho spins our thread on her loom. You are the chaste nymph, following Artemis' nature that I gaze upon as you bathe in a cool spring hidden from all but mine eyes enraptured. I hunt in deep woods where you hide from me, till at last I see, a beautiful nymph naked, running with her comrades free. Laying low in high pond grasses, my desire burns watching you skip playfully; unburdened by love's catastrophe. Revealing myself as a true lover spying amongst branches, asking to intertwine my love with thee, you run away. I am Pan, and forever you are the pipes I play. Now atop a jagged mountain, adamantium chains pinning down my will. Me, punished Prometheus, here I lay ill. I stole the fire of her beauty to warm my cold heart. Zeus' eagle and its brazen claws dig at my liver, as black as your unamorous heart.

If you are not worthy of my smile, I deem you an enemy. In any heart as clay as mine, molds lose form in time, and love as feigned as humankind shapes reconciled enmity inside. What heart could not be swayed, where the brave Perseus had once flied, but a giant now stone made eternally to hold up the sky. Or how the nightingales most beautifully sing where euphonic Orpheus' bones reside. Even Narcissus, who loved a reflection that led him to his demise. Echo's voice, riding on chords strummed on Gaia's bones do not lie. Hidden love is sacred; it cannot be despised. A heart in love sculptured from the marble once should not touch chisels again. Lest it be that love once created erodes away; a sphinx desolate in the sand, it fades away into a somber shade.

I turn to the muse of love and beauty, and in ink I am scorched as Venus denies me. Ominous weather forebodes in a pitch black sky above. Phorcys' daughters' statues root themselves on land where veins of mortals drained to a pallid tone, when eyes glanced on a gorgon, scaring skin into stone. Fog wraps between the few calm willows whose seeds being stolen by Aeolus, buried in this dark land, shed tears like the timeless figures with horror on their fleeting faces, forever frozen they stand. Hades receives them on the misty Styx, and eternally they stay after grim death takes their hand. For the willows and the dead, all is lost. Lasting is the next dying man. The son you bore, Venus, aims not at me. When shall he fly? This shadowless emotion inside beats in the heart where love battles to stay alive.

Oh muse, give me the power to cry on lines the words I soothe. My soul lacks a solid ground on which I lay you. In the rose clusters, beneath the thorns with affectionate awe, we come to bury your soul which now in heaven, lives on like the fruit that trees bear, and when life ripens them full with the spring air. Speak to us like you always did yesterday. Tell the breeze what you wish to say, so prayers may hear your voice, and consecration will fade away our pain. Our reverence is imbued to you here, on this beautiful sunny day. May your shelter be the tidings of a peaceful sleepy caress, and always hold you in our hearts, so that memories we keep of you stay the best. At last you are home after a long day, and can make time for rest in a leafy shade.

Everything like the flower needs time to bloom. Love is but another rose in the garden, but once planted, it sprouts too soon. Time is an effervescent flow where under love, it dwells. It means nothing but that we grow old, and from numbers comes nothing but the highest hell. To calculate where time goes or what numeral is the end of what we know. Oh, but only one with a taste for writing feels the truest love. Is it for my poignant reverie or for beauty in skin alive, where my deepest passion has its roots in life? But both are one. This is the truest truth of all. The leaves of love die, but with glory and love, and loved time, words, like expressions, dim under the torrent of emotion, where still in a picture of her beauty, does rhyme create life.

The querying eye which I hold not just in my heart, but in my mind, finds in worshipping what one knows they are controlled to believe. Love for a higher god than man is that brainwashing substance ravaging souls, with their pitiful wishing to conceive. God is in true love, where two hearts in rhythm beat as one above. But love is god, and even gods need love. Man is god that needs to mate like two doves bonding in peace alone. When love lives, it needs not to be asked why. It breathes one way, with two lungs. So it goes, that love lacking the airs of emotion makes life die a hundredfold. Heaven is fast, hell is slow. To some, with death is an escape from hell, this life, living with bodies we call souls. The grave, but not its contents are dead. Like past true love meets death with a rose at its pinnacle of being old, it finds a way of being remembered, so pitiless ones don't forget the way ones died long ago. My two eyes see with one heart into her soul. A grand army orderly marches before a sky full of spears launches the attack. In reverie, when the actors of words perform their act, the audience is that sweet rhyming applause that always cheeringly answers back.

On her tender wings of love I took flight, and rose up to a zenith of sensuous plight. For her I picked the fullest rose, its scented petals invented by nature and its host, the force that man has called love. It cannot divide the lioness from her cub, nor a dove from a dove. It stalks stealthily, catching its prey in strong jaws. A loved one struggles with meager attempt, surrendering to nature's law, that everything hunting passion must face true or despised love from the object with which it is enthralled. Love bites the tail of the snake, its venom poised to make pains before death's call. The serpent twines around love in retaliation, and love chants a primal lull, that since love has been known, puts to sleep the deadliest foe. But why make pain and envy rest, when the bit serpent mothers a brood of hate in its nest. Hate is that flaring creature when born, living long and hot like the sun. It melts love down to the nakedest scorn. Once cast, it makes people die in a heart stone to the core. Even the innocent apple is poisoned, either in sweet envy, or bitter love. Though any picked red fruit to man has no thorns, we are pricked in nakedness by a creature regarded as a demon seed since primal lore. And so, the hissing of the cursed snake with its forked tongue follows with the lyre's song. Either to chant yearningly to a death, or in love's silence, wait for a death too long.

Without love, one is embittered quickly with time. For anything
that loans itself to living, with the speaker becoming the soul and
listener being time, loathes without worth if love to them is not
kind. If only a lover's loved one could see that true rich ore of the
heart in love. The core cannot be mined by more than one miner,
and rare it is to see that two mines are traded for the other, to find
a choice diamond in rough. Constantly I dig to find that kind of
lover.

6/10/98

Ardent love shakes the earth violently, but time roars forward, and
reflections reveal wrinkles silently. It is indeed a quick ride, but far
from the end. That quake of love overpowers time, death ending
life but never within us everything.

As the winged creature flies by, I am angered with fury as a stampede of rage rampages on as I lie, not in my pen but in my blistered life. The ache acutely pounds until I am full of hell, and wings cannot sprout; not from my earth dispelled. Seeing the lush green brush calms my hidden ways, and chokes time's neck so that my trespassed head assails the foolish strain, and a disillusioned clock which now pokes its dastardly face at my wail. Posing its horns with mine, I charge at its final say and it rings in accolade at my dying day. Die time, so that I may live life. The people here survive in their strife. Let me forget their always assumed scythe and my own, and make hell of not life's trial, but only wicked death alone. It is that deserved time's gift that hinders the stagnantly chained poet. A creature wickedly flying by in wishing glory infinitely foretells itself, to disavow an end and destroy any hellish shrine. A spawning fish, it proliferates in springs of religious sin, and cures in its way all that is well and its kin.

But what skin can I touch that is not mine? My own bareness holds vanity up in a column twenty stories, all but empty. What detours lead to my domain, where the female bond with male thought binds to form one, a shared love the same. From where but in the trees, does my nakedness end? Not only in spirit and vision, but in my pen. We name our spirits in silence. And a column built is one with everything doomed to fall again. The temple of our belief is crushed, but rebuilt when silence befalls the fighting man. From where I go is the dry land after a long voyage home. I am free of skin and treading peacefully with free feet in the sand. Oh but love, the red fiend that squeezes my heart tightly. Another heart would make it beat so harmoniously. But my pace is slowed by my unsightly eyes and what they behold – my cherished love for a girl. Sacred to my sighs, and unwilling lovers perfect to fit in graves as skin molts off the hourglass, deceiving two pairs of decaying eyes. I can still see, and my column in hope stays empty. Pleasure, pain; you are amenities to a friend, one whose skin weeps of joy, but very truly cries in the end.

The petals reflect wishful love, but its colors when picked turn to gray when luck seizes hope as a buzzing bee searches for a brightly adorned cup. The wall of fragrant bubbling yellows keeps a mask over black ivy, sweeping the underbrush to sweetly hide love's true dark side in vanity. But where ivy grows, flowers find their way to mingle in vines to brighten love's inevitable dark glow. But for me, the sun brightens my love even more, which darkens ivy's tint and still blooms petals which offer love forever more.

A Seed's Destiny   6/21/98

The swirl of revelation is held constricted, kept low and still, and an oak's trunk is lifted to plant a new origin of religion. A sprout thunders up, calling forth the stains of another man. If somber air of a ritual makes bones breathe again in burning with fire, yet not with the passions that nature can, the needles of pine are smoothened 'til the ends. Then the dew that once knew the stem no longer waits to fall anymore again, when love and life is scented by the now ashen needles, but do not burn out till a prick of your hands does it lend. This angel fakes the eyes, but lovably so. It awakens that seed planted so god watered and thundering up. Then once a tree in bloom, now a tall branch with the axe apart of its doom. The swirl of lightning revels as the earth and love recycle their inevitable tune. The two die at different ends. One end remains dead and the other becomes it too soon.

I'd like to live in a place I've never been, awake within my mind and solemnly praised even if I lacked my gesture of skin. The sand blows away my hope, and only shells wash up, bearing knowledge of land far away I do not know; in this I cannot cope. Holding onto where I am only brandishes exotic stems everywhere I look. I walk with that effervescing river, in hers or mine, and foliage amasses thicker, with roots clumping up behind. There is no place better than my native brush, a jungle shrine that knows no time. This place has its evils, for I created it. So death includes rhyme, all before and after our passion is lit. Love is a raft flowing to my home; deceitfully built as it is, I travel with it all in hope.

Time extracts love like dew nectar but embittered with obligation. And I feel it again; what power over me controls my writing hand? Never will I relinquish love for sand within a death glass, or any token traded to amend deals of an always sad end. Austere and carved in wind and rain, an old tree before its dying day was once a sapling in its youth. Now sunken into the pitied asunder of two deaths - one in the blossom of youth, and in the fall of death into an overshadowed stump, a forgotten shade. But every leaf can only fall from its father once. Goodness forgives too few times, and bad intention grants the wish seen in an evil seed never kind.

A Specter's Path   6/25/98

When another distaste comes along, there is an equal hate hidden
in love, so that all that joins a bond can finish the dark, long before
vanquished song. The specters sneakily hiding behind natural
shades I equip against, as eyes always are felt upon me, gazing past
my neck. Their ranks are wonderfully infinite, and although I see, I
dare not look back. An idea not made faces a mirror image of one in
vain, and facing myself I force my ancient succor to deign. Pity is
wept by the scowling rain, falling with the drizzle in my sky of
clouds that holds fires no monsoon could drench to calm passion
and separate death from love and life's flame. Where does this go,
and to what end? When will I know that the flame adjusts to my hot
heart untamed, and in a bitter blend.

                                                           6/28/98

Calmer wind greets my time, but I discover that lacking the parting
hand and the unrestful shoving, it pours these spirits of liquor and
life into a goblet sipped rarely, since my taste has come to know
every seasonal strife. The spirit in a mood is a different cup; a glass
within reflecting out. The chalice bubbles reddish wine and its
contents flow in me, and I cannot be filled unless the castle built
around my binges and restraint keep a moat of love in fair amount.
So building walls high makes privacy, but calm wind brushing
against my back like against a fiendish pirates sail as he buries his
gold on land and hastily covering his tracks, holds love, life, and the
lyre in others. And they must remain in my soul sincerely that.

Words in love painted in color are red like the rosy hue of her skin. But in mine, it grows greener in watering the lover. Blood of yellow poppies fill the soul's river spread out bank to bank to grow and give to beauty's fingers. The carnal rain keeps a rose red, and fragrant words like ivy climb walls to see a bloom of wilting red flowers, where love has fled in her glower. A river erodes the wall, but words greened by light molts petals red to pale. So loved words are only red within a green skin, lonely but frail. Unseen flowers inspire my painted words, but unplucked and dry so they shall end in this tale.

7/3/98

And if pain's breeze wears our mortal cover by and by, make with the fish, how it darts smoothly away, or find one of a many demise. It isn't over, it is only one end. An end of many we must attend.

7/7/98

Give me everything, though I am feared to have that said. Mix the best with the best, and not a thing but the worst has fled. Give you religion, steal truth in exchange. Now you have an excuse for the whimpering of men and their blames. I love a thing to love all. Your truth comes before, so with all things, but your money confuses my love. I think not that I am seen in the dark. Eyes battle even without light. Only in spirit, death to sight, are they right. The light shines, and the victims are made. Conflict lies in me, my raid, sucking creation out to live in a happy dismal fade.

7/9/98

His disturbed sleep chants the song of an unpacified death.
Remnants still are contained within my soul's unrest. Tormented
through pain of my own, reflected by a cage of hell and a failing of
his life's tests. I wish to burn his death away, so that pain existing
cannot steal into another's through his unknowing anxious bane.
Inseparable ties turn my inspirations to instinctive lies, and force
out control in my pure hate and furious sighs. What rest or love can
this come to execute? All of mine. May words destroy the folly of
innumerable hells that a living dead brings alive.

7/12/98

What can you do, where can you go. The only thing I trust here is
my soul. Even as a grey leaf tumbles from the left, what humbleness
parts our waters, none on our clef. Though I know we have shown
no honor between us, this sun is brighter than both the pacification
of hope and the lack of love that both of us share. Nothing loved
you wrote. And keep your death, so love a thing you haven't even
met. Death sings a song for you wonderfully, and this world is but
dead to one buried under it. So set the example fool. I will not live
within love you know not how to keep and make callow. My hate
hides in words you bring I will not follow.

I see these thorns once more, but burning enough indeed rids a thing of its hate, love, and greed. That rose so poignant in its silent melody cut of black blood, finds the fire when its own flame has burnt out. Everyone carries a cross without scorch, but either pain takes remedy for all, nail or torch. Love's lost vigor finds strength in its sealed ways. My love is draining, and I must find hope in the words toiling within my flame.

I love the feeling in awe, and caring about the best of friends before the object that keeps me busy each day blooming, without any flaw. The toys we play with reflect the people I want to love. I love inspiration and women in general, but my red heart cannot bleed fully without giving my feelings to another for them to quell and lull. We feel different apart, but the same together. My feelings mix for everyone; good, bad, and kind. All is good so long as I can live and breathe, to taste my free rhyme. I love thee, muse. Do not fail my heart. I will pour my very blood into your vacuum until I am split apart. But obligation and time holds me back. I will love thee forever, and as we are one, we shall always live happily in pure truthful awesome love under the bright basking sun.

Love; I have no more. I wish I had given it to the thing truly I hellishly desired to have, than to foolish loving words that once I could, but no more can I adore. What can I do but love my hate and seize my death sentence, closer and closer I creek towards the door. But why must I face a fake reality that comes only once within a life, we see it as part of our soul. Death; it holds no rhyme. In itself is but unknown lore. I have sadly and hatefully destroyed my ultimate love. There is not a dove that shines white above. My eyes see no light through fissures lacking planted seeds once watered with good life and poignant love.

Life is now over for me; I cannot sew words into a colorful array of life, and I cannot love what I desire, instead of a comforting soul who wishes they were my fire. I cannot excite flesh anymore; my words discontinue the riotous parade of life that I want to live. But I must breathe, and hold my heart to try to love something I cannot reach. Hell, my friends, you do not know. Sit in a room away from dreams we wish, but cannot live to be one with them, just as tall. So I cut my body into two and I leave myself, the bad side I want to rest in a tomb. My cross is built even if I'm not ready for my death, but living dead breaks down everything. My truest love too soon, the rhyme's wrath of phantasms now past.

Sacrificial Longing   7/20/98

If I cannot have what I want, then let my soul be melted, ripped apart. I cannot live in heaven when hell always gives me an untrue and unreal fairies hand. Untrue love never real, so I stay unwell in another's dying hand. Crying love hates that words must touch hope that will never find and reach a magical braided rope. Lost in a death wishing song, my light turns dark. Truth has no meaning, and so it does, as it's false. But oh, my tear wets the catapult of journeys unknown to one, to all. My longing feels that flower I once held, I wished could grace the hand of my love dead in my world. But as I'm hated, so my love tries. But loving words are dead compared to my only true love, the only thing that keeps me living life.

The only true love is lasting. A turtle cannot die and rest until its shell is cracked. Love that will not die when a shell has been removed has flesh burning without its cover. Revealed, it lacks its true mood. The true hermit begging begs not for a shell, but its mood splashed by waves burning without seaweed nor fish to see or tell. High love is known only to one, never to two. The shell covers itself, and so does a turtle. Hermits amongst others hide not to show, but live in peace with one love, their shell alone.

7/29/98

Truth by emotion, not truth itself is where you find me. But do I dwell? I could write all day and not touch a hand. But this life would wreck me harsh if I could not love something other than a loved heart in poignant demand. Look for doubt in one's true meanings. Then you find it is real. Both sides cover one. Their reality, but love, not love enthralled. Meanings always reverse when exposed to the dank diction with which we force a soul to rehearse. My hate for love repays itself in verse. But running on this step by craggy rocky step, leaps to your emotions; none but only within a soul are they wept.

Love is so fast it stays in one spot. But my feelings melt, and in this I do indeed love for them to be sought. All that matters is to breathe you away, and not through dying lips, but the caverns of blank thought lived in nothing but a measured day. So race me and win. The treasures sought lie in the eyes, but unsearched for in the visions of our kin. Truth means zero, and so does all knowledge. For all that where we go is far better than past roads, and so, what of our soul? But this preaching never ends; all lies become eventual sarcasm in my blunt eyes. How beautiful it could be, if my tongue were properly tied to my reverie. Forsake my tongue, for I have fought the battles that the marching trumpets keep in their rung.

The Fruitless Shadow   7/29/98

In this soul, I am ready to go, but I wish I could love my truth lost in untrue hope. The air breathed keeps me dead, as long as my lungs cannot breathe close words a bird bearing leaves has said. My pain must go, either it or I. And pain as dead, yet so alive, lives to love my death so hurt in rhyme. Anymore said brings turmoil within. A human cannot weep for one so far and illusioned, so make my love dead. Please I pray god, I am alone in my heart, but so much character wild in my life brings death to love I wish to strife. No one feels words, no one knows true passion. I don't know that I love that world. The shell, she encloses me. I see and protect my soul, and it dies again without love. We tread different waters, but one ocean, for this sea we are not without. I have so much land, so much water; but without your love I am in perpetual drought.

You cannot sew without a stitch, rhyme. It becomes story lacking pleasant words coming together to form an endless marching line. My kiss wets lips of words I miss. How many rhymes, how many songs will it be, can I just have my poignant love in a body with a dash of melody? I never find it and l lose again. My game keeps one tone I cannot remove, in words or love – in both? Why is this so cruel and why must this happen? Why is this dead to a longing, but hating pen, so taking me over, I am ruled. Live, O rhyme, I tire of life. If skin cannot match our tone, leave my rhyme, keep me alone. If blood is too black to be seen, then cut me, although to unemotional terse I dare not be thrown. For all blood is black until my own veins course in one's crown; they call this their throne? But why this all approaches now, is the reason I should forget. I'm truly the blackest heart alone. It would have been a zenith, that phrase kept silent by a last ending, but what kind of taste to find I waste? O, my rhyme, I loved you as I kept you in my wake, but you fail my love that fails everything, even your own face. Past hate, far from love. I cannot kill a thing unerased above. My chalk quivers down a wretched spine. My body only barely lives, to tell of my bitter rhyme. Why must love be my theme? Why not love freed? Sorry friends, I punish you until I am bloodied by you to every end. I'm so young, but my flesh wants to leap to a pallid tone, for lived for love does not shine in any attractive sweet skin, a beauty to give me tone. Sadly only in the hell of myself, is it darkly shone alone.

You must feel something even though there is nothing to feel. And just hoping for one love to come along, mentally living in peace or hell, or physical sensuality sharing the wetness of love, proves a hated thing can be loved, and a loved thing is hated for love of peace, the opposite of war. Do not end, love. Keep moving so you can relax me in distraught, hate, and itself. But oh love, you always subtly or fully turn to hate. This is why I hate thee, but my shores dock vast ships ready to discover the gold hidden on other land, so that ultimate love is doused by another flame, and each in turn can be enjoyed, and my life will live righteously loving true love in a halcyonic female hand. By what fate from utopia am I wrest? This always is all too much. I will not ask, but try my best.

Essence in Solitude   8/8/98

Why make now a love made in so much heartache, so have me to but see through eyes punishing my way. I see through veils of love, but hated love - and wake, but only to sleep in a somber day. I rest my weariness on thorns in the many tombs I come to lay. Love does not live in the black and shadow of live fields, tinted by dark thoughts – how we feel about our life, measured by others, we turn to a dead grey. In love's liberty, made guilty by the things we say, we fall to our knees indifferent to love; and so, another day dies again. Honor your heart in its sacred land. For it does not beat simply for love, but what miles we find we travel to be freed of love's ends.

The time has come. Magic and the power of spirit have fleeted me through life's whimsical song. The dance always welcomes an excited hand left dismal without passion and the lack of romance, for poignant melody surpasses that of woman and man. A chamber of darkness, bright yet dim, seals light and abhors humans. If they could see, no one would live. Beauty, if love and thee are confusing, why must you blind my sight, and keep many to you yet only truly one reason? That destined in bitter love there is but pure treason. A glow releases life, keeping death – living in one long tone. Deep in a soul it is read, that one living dies over and over again. Power born once and never again, passed away while duties under fire are complete in finishing pity by a sharpened blade. Dance for me, with your painted hands; don't worry I'm here for you again. You are stolen of power in dance. Magic and knowledge, those only of your opposite, make sense. You are indeed none but death. In it, poignance in your romance kiss together. And frail me, I am immortal, yet rotten by your rhythm. Take my hand I will teach thee. Your hand moves spirits free to dance, making melody. But this time has come to be gone. You are in my hands, and so I shall live forever more.

When the fires of hell have burned me, and so incinerated my body be, what will be left is but poetry. It has found many ways of justice and feeling. And the only sin in me is but my unraveling cloak of skin slowly peeling. If I were murdered, then may heaven be reborn. To breathe as me, yet tender and loved, and a body free of scorn. If only meaning could come alive and find passion more toughly in hot shiver. Then in that, my dreams are real; but see them within and they wither. Perhaps if I was traded by another soul, they could see a certain devastation. My bell is rung and hate is more than welcome. Longing hurts its way inside and creeps away in poignant elevation. But shadows are my last excuse. Why profane as they are in me, and damned and fooled I am by my malady? What final praise shall I be honored into as I make a fated last pose. For on a hill hammered by rage and temptation I will stand. No stain of blood yet, only fighting hands. I throw myself into a last battle, pitched amongst the very hells of earth. To kiss my love goodbye to defeat them, in that some sense thereafter, I can be of some honored worth. And my merit and glory in thee is shown. My body's fallen along with the evils of a bloodstained earth. I shall be the fallen one, after all my good is done.

Seven weapons rip apart life in finding love, life's clever demise. Faring with love's impish ego, it seeks to imbue a heart with a handsomely crafted silver arrow. Being tipped by pure emotion, embittered love soon shall follow. The pheon opens love's gash and at some end the arrow is pulled, dripping with once loving blood. Pain buried finds a deeper wound to weep in a crying place, making dead love alive in a soul double doomed. The club of sorrow does make its rage known, when feelings forgotten well up, and a blunt force hits bones like an avalanche of stone hitting stone. Beaten love sweats blood under the swinging club. What fresh eyes to see with may come after punishment? Not one master of that weapon has ever been told. The axe of death bluntly leads opposition to rest in dreams unknown. It steals the very ripe desire of youth so bold, and heals those dying painful in love, in falling skin unrestfully cold. The dagger of hate is as sharp to a wielder as to the thing which it shall relate. Call it the perfect sidearm in the assassin's array. Piercing love is dismembered by this blade on a bloody day. Pity for those above or below this once soiled dirk seeks neutral change to avoid the wraths of this hidden blade at a later date. The spear of time holds its innocence by the victims it has carried away; no witness to its only duty. Skin in shadows of its pole it seeks to thieve with the death axe at hand striking. A sword, most tempered not by anger or whim, but love, slides straight through foes in their wrong. Revenge is bound to this blade, unsheathed to victories great. Dreamed in silence, it marks a bitter soul. But brandished after victory and chance, it is the strongest and deadliest of this arsenal; against every weapon of the world.

So cold, I am always by your side. My heart makes simple duty be unrest; why can I not find faded hope, love, and past sighs. Fantasies of her pretty face, our love together combines. But no longer can I feel that way. I'm growing steadily older, farther away from beautiful simplicity of love long ago, and sweet love that I sorrowfully cannot find again in this world. Pity for the earth or the ones above those once fallen by the soiled dirk? Answer me in my love, not in my hate. Realize when you must properly relate. For in love, you show my dark way. In hate, for some reasons love is sealed by me. I cannot love the way I meet my fate. So my sweet one, I need not taste more of bitterness. Love has been resurrected past its allotted time. Now it will not live inside or out of thee. This love I search for I will not find, lest it be that I find you in my rhyme.

Unearthly Flame   9/1/98

What might be found amongst and past the heavens, stars aflame?
The only thing on earth is love, the only thing that keeps me
contained. Put god in the sky by sacred means and bow to the air,
what lacks far away of any thought or flesh. Beautiful earthly girls
cannot be found but here, for they are the earth's passionate best.
To travel off this sphere, to spin in orbit to find love that could be
infinite like a universe, a creature more beautied by solar winds.
Celestial bodies, free in their whim. Something so great, Zeus could
not bear her beauty's strength. Words are erased in my heart, only
living thoughts of feeling remain. I left the green and sea to find in
space a lonely lady. I soar up to only be vaporized by the sun; I
again fall to earth. Here, my home. I search in this land, this world.
But hearts here are either sleeping or broken, in pity for some.
Mine own passion morphs the same. I heal my wounds by looking
up at some beauty - her flame? But I remain burning in the cold.
Pluto, too far to tell of, knows. My pyramid is built atop of the
world; I fall from above to be at rest, entombed with pictures of my
love. Why in space must gravity be the only constant? My heart
beats not for the stars. I lack the human beauty for any girl's eyes to
see me afar. Nothing exists in space, but something I cannot reach.
The only girl's lips I'll have to taste.

What Shines? 9/9/98

What the older have resurrected the young must read, and others' madness sneaks deep inside of my pen as it bleeds. I'm so foolish when life bids me well. I take solemn praise to honor it more above all, equally to it itself. I am not free just look at me. You will not find this body, for it is your trap and my own. I've lived so long in a ghost's shell made of bone. This is my battle behind enemy lines where love sacredly hides. I finish my life before my love, this thing of one rhyme and one season, of many colors. With it I am alone. So I feed my heart, stained by darkness, what I don't know. I fight myself until that shadow I can shed light upon, but it hides again to creep into my life once more. I feel doomed and with no love. Yet I love myself, the ghost whose fate is already dealt. Call me dark, but I am far beyond the fog and light, and now remain undead to taunt this life in my bitter silent plight.

It has changed in my feelings, my dark side atoning my love ensuing. At the bottom of my world my fire burns coldly, and you rhymes have changed my soul, but foolishly. Everyone steals my love, what little is left burning in the rain. I write naught for her, but my anguish, toil, and pain. And to pluck that rose, it steals away in shadows on walls I know I cannot color without simple love. A flower does not hide my love, for I traveled with it to her home. She is there, but blank to my eyes which see only hope, yet now only despair is what I know. Truly, she is but a lost soul. Soulless I am, I will be told. Love will go, and these gates shall close. Capped by demons, the opposite of love unfolds. I have lost in this life. It is so cold, and my love so old I will not strife.

9/19/98

I search myself, the ground I stroll, but the land does not fulfill my dreams; the girl I love still. What many ways down paths unreal take my heart betwixt my eye, truly blinded by this dark dream untold. Drifting with the wind, sent down by thunder. Still my ways become bittered by mine own soul I seek in plunder. I find myself burrowed in a metal rage. To lift and grow strong in darkness, still I am undead in an unholy cage. I do not run to religion, beyond my say, and hurt me further by my death as it casts a broken soul down, and I ponder as a grim figure struck by love not to gain. And I remain in this unruly seal, my soul. And still I am a cast shade; these powers befit my dying fade.

My dark heart cannot be shown what it is to love and be loved by a soul. One girl to bring me alive, no longer a toy - a puppet for their eyes. So long have I been with only hope and pitiful sighs. This muse helps destroy my insides, for love does not fade nor does it exist in rhyme or life. I seek power instead of dreams, to summon my entire empire to love thee. Yet I cannot see your eyes, so I am blind lest it be that I find you in but only rhyme. Feel these words, thou hateful ground. For I march and march to only crush and burn what I've built atop your crown. So I honor thee, most beauteous earth, and her pretty eyes will have it I am not in this world. I hear not with my own eyes, but with too forsaken a heart. Not a lion, but a crow; tattered feathers fallen by some befallen black art. But my warring foes now fall to the ground, blood stolen by my blade. I fight even in love, so I'm destined to be destroyed. I live to but hunt and raze all love to the ground. I love thee, bloodied earth, for all that is loved shall perish with you. And everything taken by temperament shall seed the quaking world, swallowing all good hearts as well.

Ghost at the Docks   9/24/98

Something safer, yet so close I cannot hold my talk with. Destined, false motifs your theme keeps. Today I am not so bold; today I weep. Yet by yesterday, I hold the sun in my breaths, for three I take, and in with thee and out with the wind. You breathe my ghost, is it not my mistake? Neither in fear nor somber pardon does my merit give thee a wave. I tangle with you 'til I am stricken in fright and destined to lose, yet it does not faulty fight. It drifts away and so by ways the ship does arrive, though I wish you to stay inside; a ghost needs time to set things aright.

Hall   9/24/98

I am solely preoccupied by this love, this blank unpainted hall. Invisible to my flow and dying maw, for I breathe a thousand words through the window to silently whisper alone. I do not have sullen instinct, but turn to a mellow tone. For when love in its breeze following song turns to heights of zenith, the all of me, I breathe wide. But my grave holds my grey death fathoms deep too young and unrested to even cry. I yearn to spin the questions on these hands that turn and turn to make my love wonder, oh wonder why. That love, you are a wink but blind to a foe. I will sing to you, but my heart has it that no girl shall ever wish to behold. So I lie on the soul, rely on the sword. Rename my love once more, breathe in, and walk down my painted hall alone.

As it was, I see our poignance as some of my own. I know what he sees, and he is sad by the way things have gone. You want to travel back, but my love would not be there at all. I'd be hurt in a love so rare now all gone. My jewel is at the bottom of the rains, a giant sea. To drift along silent I search black, foggy bog reeves. To see what I have dreamed, I must be a fish to search for you, the mermaid in ocean blue, although my love cannot be true. Stricken afloat, clouds day and night darken my humble abode. And I am wrecked into thinking my love is a pure dream, yet a fantasy unreal. The moon shows not what stars may shine down my back. For I search love but it never answers back. This day cannot live without my dream, and so it shall be that I will live in unreal reality. But I am dead; this ghost here, writing sad. I wish I was an unknowing lover as a boy, a mere lad. Oh goodbye my youth. My somber hope of love in her never came true.

Darkened Light   10/3/98

She is with me to this day, and the soul I am in I wish to stay. I mention love again and cannot stray of sorrow in your stare, and blank worlds of words kill my means and I feel your shine rare. But when the sun does come, behold how it shines bright, yet seeing love in your ways gives it more grace, shadowed darker than night. Sweet flowers die with thee in light, even on a grave they darken might. Oh how magical is your love, the thing that comforts any rest I procure. Though sleep in love I can endure. But if I wake under spell, love grants no wish, no escape. It turns to hell. Let it be that all sweetness lies in your duties felt.

Pained Distance   10/3/98

Not an idea of its thought, for love contains no feeling now, but my
soul in rot. Why research death at so young an age? My willing
body should die more beautifully, but all my tones are wrong; and
all words, they do not follow. For my death has come already. Life
was good without love, a lack of a woman's skin; one less
composure for me to solve. But the problem remains my obstacle,
and rhyme meant to destroy that. Buy in rhyme and sell my love to
lined paper. I made a duplicate of you, though I know this world
doesn't need another copy, but a future. There is relief in knowing
death with each step gets closer. The greater the detachment, the
higher the loss. The higher my indifference, the greater the love.

                                                    10/3/98

Straight ahead of me, love sits in my view. She now unperched by
my whim, my loving revenge in lieu. Does the opposite feel what
sorrows and hate, yet loved places I once knew? This is my vacant
space you plant on to grow aloof. But by unconscious ways, my love
does not sprout. My dream is awake with living, not to a sprout
ungrown and unfelt. Dreams lack in too meager a youth. Uncouth in
their true despairs, all people love without useful wishes, for theirs
is a wandering with nothing felt. The hope that dreams are theirs
makes me look upon my life as a dream from the past in which I
should dwell.

I disgrace thee; the outside powers have thrust an eye against me. For I wait in hopes to breathe amongst troubled isles of despair that you pitch and call for. A far off home with wishes and dreams plagued with scorn. I sit and cry to die in anecdote. A flowing breeze cools thy breast and reports to me that true love does find its way past death. But with one ear and eye shut seven fold, I brave the waters of love I am under now, to drown in hope? Find me naught in thine eyes, but with thy sweet sense of hearing that lies. Trick your false love and see that you lack, but your love will remain in my heart a somber black.

Illusionary Existence   10/5/98

Love has come and love has gone. But it lasts in my spoken word truly so long. Your tear appears on my face, since your words for me wither by disgrace. To truly love an angel truly devil, tricks my love to be archangel. Her love was naught, for attraction must come before and always after love is sought. Filling my eye with a teary silence of poignant sigh, I forget to love life instead of a shadow resembling her face once beautiful; now down every stairway the torch I carry illuminates a darkness in which this shadow no longer dwells. If only she knew in her words a why, then love to be could count as a find. Outside and remote in fog by trees eroded by wind and time, a character of forlorn solitude I denote. By hoist and sail from this place, my love could be you, to climb some barren rope. False loving girl, you feed my dreams and mending hand well, but my body received not thy blessings immersed by no love, and red by blood past and present within already spilt. Stay dead in yourself, and destroy feelings you know not you kill.

A Shadow in the Rain   10/6/98

Tears flood even though they don't come, and through fond
memory I am alone. But to sweat a sigh in the midst of rain on a
dark night through loyal floating feign, what befalls my truth of
love? That we are both captured by shadows: pictures of ourselves.
Through a wide torrent of some unreal fate, I condescend my
throne to be dead in the rain. Bleak by how love has been, how it
has gone. We flow within love, though I know it's not within your
soul. So by my rain I am soiled by shadow, but in your clouds I see a
sun that keeps me bold and I follow. But the story knows love that
cannot be shown or borrowed, even if lovers to be are told their
waters will be shallow. Bells mate my tone, but my love is not ours.
Truly accursed by love not known, only mine alone and callow.
Sense the tone, remarry the sword. Shadow my ways and flee 'til
I'm gone.

                                                       10/10/98

Now I travel back to those days when I felt glad I was with you, a
fleeting dream of a future. Enemies I knew not I could have. By
those ponds of youth, of greatness and honor in destiny, dead by an
unpeaceful yet calm rain of yesterday. Loved by the wind, not by
her hair, and I could stand millions of foes off with my bare hands.
This absence of sex destroys all endeavor, all love. It robs your
body, youth, and soul. Now I speak of girls, somber to me, yet
sweet; or so I am told. I could love simple young life, hard with pain
as I advance, and grow more cold in dance. My tears seal not a
rhythm, not one happy thought. Steal my all, sacred to my soul in
rot. A ghost I am, for it is not I that speaks with thee. I am you,
shan't you be me. My love extends only to one, not to all, and is in
silent, blessed memory. Though love, I can feel my young body
rotting.

And so I end with a blasphemous struggle until the days of tomorrow. This weeping can end, along with my love I sought in sorrow. Join me Kim, for I am plagued by your flower, the flower that he could not give. So sadly I drift away. I cry not for myself, but this love I trust you have not felt. A ghost in many ways I am, but only by love. This love I feel for you, only you. But I am punished by my unwilling tone. For the flower I held glows terror. The way I could not have it left on the right home. Goodbye Kim, but I'm still alone.

Fading into Fate   10/10/98

I see you again, and I try to find you although I have lived as I am dead. I want to touch again, to feel this glow. But I am saddened unto death, for you breathe no more. I hide away by sacred means, and my hope is nothing. Rhyme has died with you, and so I am but a shade shattered by nothing but dead dreams and a lack of fantasy. I died for you in the attacking, and I still sing hymns of praise as a ghostly light. Sirens could not please my ill-tempered sight as others tore out my eyes. I am tortured even feeling rhyme. Oh hate. But love, no! I cannot love anymore. My drained stalagmite pit contained within is filled with horror by a hate I so adore. I hate so much, I now hate everything, and all is unborn. I erect no flag, no place of honor. On the edge of nothing I cower. The changing of hate inevitably wants to be neutral in our determined hours.

Final First Hope   10/10/98

This sway of passion branches to emotion, a rampant rapture in
pleasure knowing no other. I came to see if my love still haunted
my roads of the past, albeit false, while repenting my actions for
years to come. But what of truth? My sight can only go so far. And a
blur after, sends me to my world. Your vision, my strength.
Together what love could come at length? But in this room, it is
dark and dreary. You are the wind I cannot breathe of, and in
breathing, I suffocate in woe. My hope and dream tears down walls
between our love.

                                                         10/10/98

I pick this pen because it haunts me in the way I share my love
unannounced to the world and sea. I cannot piece together these
broken fragments of stained glass again. To do it once shall suffice
amidst my sin. To compile your love in one simple book leaves me
bound to my chains, so I am unfree to find hope. Where was this
book I made, and how is it so, that when I look in the puddle I see
beauty, but death that taunted once and now remaining long. It was
her shiny hair, her voice that lacked any love. I hate to rip my lungs
out, but I feel alive yet honored by my wrong, that love for me
exists in my plain song.

In a wave of bliss, love cannot miss. Over a ravine I stare, and love could be in this air. I grasp my sword and tilt my glove. Oh how sweet she was when we were in love. The sun slowly rises up. How did I find in my life such a time to have such luck to find myself. Still I stare at a picture in time, her beautiful golden hair. Waves of darkness I see now, and wave at comrades close in sound, realizing I've lost the one I love. By silent plight in illusions of love in myself I now only find. My duties, they compare not to love, but my shattered soul enslaved by unworthy wealth. Clad in armor after a long battle to only return to ruins, I sift through the remains of love. In the fallen remnants I dwell.

Do not lend your eye to darkness,

For it takes not a hands grace.

By writing in light, my sorrow debts can be paid.

Sap off my joy, but live youth in rot,

Beside a lover's grave.

Pay off with less taken, and regard with less esteem,

That love straight through all my time knows not of time's breeze.

I must foil my thoughts by cautious love.

In this, I procure myself to only but a comfortable old age, beside empty wealth.

Unreal Reflection   10/13/98

The writings of wraiths and abstractions borrow another's love, for
the lack of my reaction. To see her flower, how it blooms every day.
Between my heart and hand, somber unto love I am, for the soil
does not dampen in my land. I plant with drought, containing
myself with outright sorrow. Enjoy love from a third person point
of view, instead of first hand. Find my mirror and be vain, in vain
looks borrow love at another price of love already paid. In this, all
of my complements come at the cost of thine eyes, whose fitting
know not love, but the luck of another love's dice.

                                                       10/13/98

The squirrel finds first simple reason to mate his girl. To chase
around trees gives good exercise, yet humans have not their whys.
Emotion takes the place of natural selection in a race to find
companionship, love's unknown direction. She feeds her willing
ways by my youth, money, and taste. I know she lacks my reality of
hate, love, and seeing willing beauty unraped. So I hate thee in
disguise, and instead of useless sighs, I falsely mate the closest
angel lacking these whys; a bitter end to one wanting to coerce the
unwilling virgin delight.

Remembering my love so long, I am painted by you as a dismal shadow. Or is it that I'm marked by love, the unpainted memory lacking the fruits of my sorrow. Both sharp edges not having bled twice, both sides love not in me to pour an ounce of right. Calling for the shadow to raise me again, I named this child "Romeo" to pay for my sins. Thus, I am tricked by my own satire, fate for my poor soul to lend. Call me in love a dreary sight, drenched by sorrow of loves light: lies by her beauty's whim; I am killed outright.

An End Denied   10/20/98

Mourn my days as a youth, to grow old young still ripe with pain in love I never knew. So end, yet you will not. My wish depends not on my soul but my body that cannot rot, twisted towards love never to come true. But then I've done the wrong things too. "Do you have a death wish?" speaks a reaper. "Are you its granter?" I reply. "You cannot attest to death so young. First you must make more trial of pains on earthen land. This way I will be sure that thou art dead." A casket would not be vouched, nor deserved even with paid toll. For restrained love thinks it still has the right to decay my soul.

With this mask, I can talk with you forever. Without it, for you to see me would split this body by a cleaver. Tell me, is it love you sought and still seek? Is it already found, and if so I must forsake my weep. You were the blamer of love, the chosen one. Still, I cry on blank lines always blunt. You poisoned my pen, my veins, and my heart. Take your little wings and ignore my finding eye. And if you dare speak of hate, I must now part in sigh. I want to know, who was the framer of your love? What clever hands wove its rug? You do not know me. You know a speck of the past, for that child is dead. Now you are behind my insidious laughs. I will cry over love I missed. And not a wink now could hide my willing youth amiss. You shall live, and I truly shall die. Amongst my burning love, my death wished cry. You may hate me now, but I love you proud. Still I am forever more in love with your shroud. Forget me, but do not destroy my hidden wealth; the only half in dreamed love, the only part that matters now.

10/21/98

We all seek the darkness for different reasons. One love for me drowns my empty seasons. And the tomb of an empty year, an empty life, tricks love betwixt my rights. So court my love, for you are the judger of yourself. I can cry during sworn affirmation, but my hard trials are heard better by tears, than by all worser company. You insist upon me, to gather evidence that mine eyes do not judge thee. You are dismissed, love. But gather around fools of the jury. Love is in me; but with her and her eyes, they did not see their simple testimony.

Dream on the Frozen Summit   10/21/98

Atop this summit, my sexual peak, the horizon meets the lonely sky
in the company of no sun. And the ground weeps snow melt in a
long sigh. My warm tears, down a steep slope run. To climb down
off this mount despairs my sense of self. My lack of height, and
unruly love. To reach up to another summit, one more journey,
would keep me warmer. A ground freezes my sight. All emptiness is
alive, and I am ice. Despite my cold hope, a frosty path could lead to
some paradise, beyond this dead slope. But to be that high again
would temper my fall. How low the cliffs are, and how grand is my
loss; all I confide. Love loses sight, and I am blind.

                                               10/21/98

If I look at thee I feel I am rotten, all bad. And as always I look away,
happy for nothing but only poignant memory. I rejoin myself
sorrowfully sad. I only pronounce myself, since I am at the will of
your flogging. But thine eyes knowing not pain or torture, they to
me have dealt. Oh, I suffer within. Why can't I make clear my love I
see not, nor can I say. So I am the fool, jestering the fellow man.
Toying with love of any girl, her eyes she unknowingly lends. So as
a clay heart, my will shapes with thy looks. And with sad
languishing faults I end for good.

After climbing so far to see an end of this endless storm, a fight ensues in the rain - two parts battle, belonging to one. Crossing this pair under a sacrifice do two deaths play a part. And fog and wind rids us of the wretched creature, fallen by my storm. The two unblemished shoguns do fall before their rise, and face off, all in black adorn. While frozen and locked in time, she stares above. And fire lights the canopy before the sun. Land turns to destruction, and the ground slowly rips up to the sky. An untimely demise, for the earth now is torn from all eyes. By fate and honor's blade, one dies, the other to fall brave. His sacrifice lies in the sky, and I take his hand, for he is part of mine. With our battle finished, the ice of her beauty melts, since she was an angel now fallen from high. "Before thou art frost and bitter gone, kiss thy lips before I am stone." By my parting last we are locked, now opened by a dawning sun. I barely kiss her lips unparted, and my soul slows to poignant rot. Frozen as I, she untaintedly freezes to die. I approach a ledge of these lasting high stone walls by a green bog reside. Unsheathe thy sword! But by fire of sky, a parting yawn, this gauntlet reaches for the sun. By pulling this edge, my fate is done. And so she lies in a bed of frost, eternally solid. I stand alone, facing a sun that turned me to stone. But over a closing eye, and death coming soon, I wait for the cliffs. Oh! How beautiful love has been, how it looms all alone. And this world remains for no one to roam. We are ice and stone, and the dream is gone.

The greatest innocence suffers in time with the strongest sin. One not cleaned nor purged, a constant pain within. I relive a day in one true loving hour, thousands of millennia away. And I rest to die in myself, the way I respect love; it cannot find a girl with pure truth in itself. I could lie to thee and say my feelings are wrong, and I am a glutton for sexuality. But it is better to die than to face unanswered love. My horrorful ghost in hell, it lacks any angel, now being dark. And I will live the same forever more unwell.

I cannot live in this putrid body, a soul without any reading. I rest but wake. I am asleep as the day and wake at night, since my eyes in light know only fright and many a girl's deceitful eye. It's between my hate and love, existing hate again, something that does not face the sins of my love I cannot win. I can fight with the greatest heart and the strongest man alive, but I'm dead unto love, for the battle is my life. So read her soul, do not become a vampire, old before your youth. It pains me so, that I must grow old before I can know love. For only in stories is it told in parable, in some paradise after you die, in the clouds above the fields of my simile, it tells that those without love, they cry. The story isn't through yet, but I know clouds. They cover a sun as a gray reminder of love's empty past. I will live in this rain, for this sin unto myself clothes my back, and the depths of this flood drowns all hope of love, a drowning of the soul in suffering wrath.

All is the beginning, for creation created man. Null is the end, where souls stopped beating then. Sap is the tree that hides us to see our every move, and while hiding we see us in our every mood. Lack the eye of the fellow man, and rid myself of the evil emanating from their silence of hand. Paint whim by another method, and take another soul lent, never given. Mold the soul to the proper shape, and weed out its disgrace. Then you find it shall deflate.

Listen fools! Do not follow thy lady's hand. For only in her love is it safe then. Beat in your being's rhythm. In this, she can't catch you in your run, to hide where you can't be found. Death seeks to steal a youth so poignantly loud. Weave with cautious fabric, not anything different than thyself. Kiss thy love, kiss not yourself, unless wretched arrogance is more blessed, and wished to be felt. Sadness tricks a man, especially in love, where all fiends are uncovered and monsters are born. Seek in her a feeding soul, a filling, not dour mouth. In this, love is secure in her luscious mounds – not in a beauty who doth lack emotion, nor soul abound. Take in pride thy love, show thy hands who it doth truly adore. And friends, call her by a sweet name, the one she always goes by. But share not dreams, only if you in her find. Share wealth even, and part with thy sum of things. Bless her love, but bless not thy rings, nor love in counting. Dye yourself by your favorite colors and be real to the extent of only yourself; not thy soul, whelp! Rest in death, and die in sleep. But even though feigned love is a parting wish, let it not be thy dream. Last but not least, choose not a girl who cannot fill in thy blanks, nor one without a parting thanks. Bless my wind, I am gone. Shatter not love, but thy mirror in scorn.

I feel so cold at my love I cannot bold. Oh my love I've sent stricken, painful in my view. I am ice, cold by your loving, and my soul that never knew. Your warmth is the only thing that might persuade me. That a kiss in love could be that much more, than lips I bite in scorn. Oh, dismissed hate! A hate for myself that I cannot call love. I love thee, and in that you keep me running away. Oh, by my mistakes you keep me wrong. And by love I cannot fill, I wish with you to be so long. I am cold, and cold I am by my grave. For you show no happy interest, whilst my burning desire enrage. Oh hark, these false loves I denote; only for you I wrote. Oh take my death, take this hand, this rotten hand, for I cannot love anymore. For thy finding famine, always unfeeding my soul, yet you in your beauty, your golden hair, captivate myself by winning your love that I cannot have with you. No human dies, yet fades away in these waves, my empty say. You are crystallized by these whys. My love, I cannot think nor reason; sad is my little heart, the dark side is all I am. Your ways I wish to defend, but alack I am to love the thought of loving my offend. I cannot face you, for eyes for me know only love to thee one true. But I will die with this unfed soul; my love for you. This thing you don't know.

You found me at the right time, but the wrong age. And now alone, I splash my guilt of everything, my guilt of love all enraged. Peace I do not find, lest it be that love awakens the day. So I run with scope, and caress the rhythm after long years in a never ending rain, yet still I am pondering hope in conquering pain. Alas, my crime remains always the same. I'm blasted with deeds I cope, yet killed by love every way. Sorry love, I abuse your every tone; the one that sings somber, in longing for time - the time of love all gone. These lies I hold in love paint my skull all in doom. Scythe my neck, and love might disappear, becoming this tomb.

10/30/98

It was not love that captivated my soul, but love for the demons, whose rhymes kept being told. Now I part with something always a part of my ways, but lack the conscious belief to foretell a new lover's face. A sullen black crown does every hawk carry, every raven, a silver thorn. With wolf-like grace my flower bleeds now not by love she created, but I stubbornly adorn, razed and unfound. So drought, pick not this season to abuse; for I am well watered by love for my muse.

And so by my muse I am born. This life tickles my imagination, and laughs down on the waves. My wealth counts not as dollars in the sand, nor love I plague by wait and song. Instead, my love makes more time than I can expect. Riches of pure love could be what would soothe this roaming man. The beach sand hides so much, covering all that is left by waves; shells, treasures, and dreams in time by zooming days. But if passion can calm my winds greater than earth's by your leave, I might find carnal passion greater than my way of love – I look before I leap. Utopia cannot be found in you or I, but between our heart and sigh; and my unknown lover's eye beside.

The root of the tree shows not its strength, but a past unwatered as the mood lacking seed. At least air is fresher by waves of composure, if a muse could sing. Oh I lack the abuse or pain of scorn anymore. If only I was in love with a beautiful girl, instead of one love I mourn. And those fruits of life I seek to pick are unfed by this tree – they live unborn. If my riches were equal to that of my soul, then so shall my love become peace sought, but still unsewn. I untied jauntingly elope. So water thy trees and drink in your love, even though it lurks not in thyself.

I've waited so long for you my love, the one I adore. Cherished in my heart, yet took revenge dipped in your blood. Thank you for sharing a bitter soul. I survived the darkness to destroy one illusionary love, dead I felt so long. I hamper not one feeling enraged. Now I can rest in my soul unscathed, still to age. My love was lesson in the dark blood I swam, always in your grave. My honor is taken and now my soul must reawaken to be saved.

I've wasted so rich my youth to a thieving soul I cannot lose. So, damned hell, die by yourself. Do not let me fall again to thy fiendish muse. But alas it is her soul that cannot be fed. Thus in this I feed only my own. So now I am only dying beside a soul unloved and unshared to the end alone.

I only romance this angel. This love I've felt so coldly, yet so bold. If my tongue could sharpen my lies even greater than my endless sighs, my love could be what would open a hole, darkened by my pain and tears in the sky. Oh, ethereal love is never known. It is only left within a soul in dreams unknown; drowned and battle-torn as a sinking ship with too many riches to count, so many bars of shining gold. Love cannot wait beneath my depths. It must bloom, and only to her I can have that shared. Though now I am belittled to be known. I remain a ghost. My eye has seen so far in life; many a place, dead rhyme. Oh her pretty face! My ruins are burned to find you in my life. This maze I dwell, I need you inside. But wicked torment breaks my bitter soul. And perchance, gamble if I may, love for you means nothing, since life cannot say. Oh if only my wounds could be found in you. And love then for thee would stain true. But as a wretched, weak, deadened soul, it feels as If I shall die with love for a shade. But alas, it is your love to harp on my grave. I indeed wish on everything in the galaxy could move our moon; to eclipse against the hot sun unmoved. My tomb is this soul, ever since you found me prime and lone. Love, I wish you could comprehend my love to lend. My deep spirit locks my heart to find you again. And I will not give nor give up love; you are my only end.

I have so much love, but I can't spend it now. Thoughts had I, for I was proud. Without any soul's clothing to shield me from the times of wind, I suffer dearth and pine within. This bark echoing from wolves through trees will not howl, but my cold heart shall remain painful and hurting in my world now sorrow. Why must one so enriched with a poignant hand march and restrict love – it shall not answer back. I loom truly in this life in meager cry, and my soul shall ask the same question: why? I understand not of thee, only myself. And no dreams come of this; I hold only empty wealth. By a false muse in a wandering bliss I am unfelt. My lady's hand, the one I've made in there, mixes my blood with struggles felt enshrouded by a cape, cloak, and hood. And still bare and unwell forever before myself I am knelt beside thee, and cannot find truth in dreams unreaped. And so I continue, to find what lies in the misted fog ahead for me, and find nothing. Lest it be unto love my own dreary eyes could see, my fake tears on my soul do feed.

Research evil to know what is good. But your deceit shows not love nor hating as it should. Trading its seedless vow as a lie, it heads the mast as the corpse of the captain at its bow. The rest of life shows not in the wind, but it is now alone and unproud. Give up on silence to face an endless song, as my love does not reach to her, for she sings quietly in my perpetual storm. In the crow's nest the sail sets high. With strong wind and poignant eye we shove off to lands where still my life remains to show her what love could be if she and I were beside. But my end will not show thy planks who it doth walk, for strong jaws will not confess my poor body to talk. In the waves on this soon departing shore, your pretty silk all reddish with luster shows not your forgiving nor a giving love, but a fantasy tricked still I muster in resembling tone. In thy beauty, I am your woe. But no love shared nor told. And in a dead wish, this world warmed by love stays cold.

Your love lurks in your trees I roam. I swing about in love but find no water or loving home. So filled with ordeals of despair and a parting soul freshening the deedful air. My melody ripens youth, but tricks my fear I game to dare. So if my hopes are out of reach, but as high as this love I find so rare, let me find that tone of picturesque beauty amongst thy sweet sounds bare. Rotting fruit does not flock the wild beasts. Even to pick flowers of love in the cool breeze amongst jungle cantaloupes in the canopy of trees makes me invisible as the wind. But finding your hope is but a quarter turn of your own hair, so love may very well fly to thee if you are to be heard. Pain tops all of sorrow, and endings have one-way crossroads. The clouds rest over sleeping toads. Love's entire field reaps spring's color of fragrant flowers all in daunting rows. Pick a muse and make it sing, the echo is the answer to the way life should be.

A bitter past is a bitter fall. In thy love you bloom this cold rose alone. The muse I make unto this shall only appall, and my willing love I breathe won't catch me as I fall. So a better future depends upon the last test, to see if you are capable of handling thy guest, lest it be that I could forget. To see a charge and new beginning, for our love cannot darken to my eye, so between us my love can only be shown as a sigh. So I rest in deep sleep, beside no waiting beauty as I atone in dreams far off, unreachable alone. I come to remark a silence long felt, come now to be gone. Only in silent woe no one knows, a secret that appears to lack in man even if shown. I diminish love to be burning in thorns I sharpen by my stare. No words can explain the rose that is you, always fair. If I could water thee, it would be in a muse. Making seeds with the words watered by a temperate rain that could live in you. Though I know how new lovers are shy till they've mended their roots, and tasted each other's fruits. In this land I thought was ours, flowing and loving rivers cascade not inside of you or I, even if it's so, in this endless forest of somber silence, of dreams willed by the maker of the fall.

Since calling to love in bad ways we part alone, apart in our fade. A somber soul lurks if not in the sorrowful heart, then thy lover's breast aroused and beating. This spirit judges me in this room by a mere lot of space, and time's dignity always knows not of disgrace, or love to bold. So by feathers all in flight, all of my hopes eroding and ending desire, they fall before this empty man's tormented height. And beloved, I wreck the beauty of us within your eyes, that finds not one ounce of right. Darkness lurks in halls of sorrow, a torn friendliness I cannot strife. Not by yesterday or tomorrow, for your will remains callow, our time as spirits here passed by.

The Monarch of Sorrow   12/26/98

Disappointment after disappointment, thus in this I feel appointed. And in my feigned hierarchy I truly can be known in my own reign as a king of sorrows from long ago, with a hearted queen boasting of her lover's fame. Although she not beside now the one love who feels as if he hasn't an antidote or heart. But in distant, ever-fading love, he cries out to above. His somber way shines through, collapsed in his throne now on the other side of cold stone walls, blocking the shine of the sun in hellish dreams so shrewd and not won. But victory is not on earth. In the heart of man only will it lurk. Sink an armada built by loving hands, and leap to death off a burning ship in faraway lands. But die knowing your gold lies not in holes in mud, but so much for lovers now dead in the flood. And my sorrowful kingdom is ruled by the dying monarch, though not for good. Words are a curse to a feeding and willing lute that jests as a fool. A somber baron even without his crown should know, that love only feeds itself between two.

I am bored yet sick unto death, that love for a ghost is my best friend. We live together and you brighten my dark days; and with your lies, deepen my false sense. Speaking to love when it does not reply becomes a simple sorrowful sigh that shall quench my heart, though even inside does it lack. And with a grant of fire, a touching soul to revamp, I fine tune a yearning love to stay as my only messenger sent. Oh, I've tricked my eyes and now all I can do is but carve a whim to your cries. You deserve the worst, yet my best to try to kill and be killed in my unrest. Do this unto love, and now it becomes a plot to research revenge. With a poignant eye I've only begun to attend to this ghost without mend. How can I help end my encounters of unrequited love? Disaster exists in your eyes, for with my soul you plunder and rob. An axe would do wonders for this glory sought, as the death of the haunts of love shall now come.

Oh love, I write to you so often. Do you deserve these words I cannot bring by sound to thee, so still remain my coffin? If my will of love could endure under the sweat of any love's pain, then wishes from my dreams would be compassion, and only the destined fate of our love would reign. I am no longer tricked by our dance. So confused I was when water always fell from above, feeding crops that withered without thy lack of sun. But oh, my weather has been turned to complete dark. Because love, you know not where to start. I feel a sorrow foreboding in these clouds I am and have followed. You are both life and death. So I detached, remain thy sweetest friend. I loved you when my muse was sharpened by your beauteous eyes, a blank wishful love as blind as mine. But now alone, I can only write ill-tempered, unlusting, unfitting for any eyes. Sorry to say my love, this cherished glory for your soul shall forever rise. My sorrow begets my end and the new spring would not allow it. Unto you I have committed so many silent sins. This rose for you bleeds now, and by kneeling, no honor will come to either of us even if the knight becomes the throne. Never will I find a beauty like you on this tumbling axis, our vanishing memory of a home.

I was in her heaven, she was in my hell. The tree of love has been watered, overflowing outside my cold realm. If I could find the words to replace love, it would be in your own beauty and unforgiving heart. I enjoy a rest amongst these leaves, for comfort comes from sorrow, not from thee. If we all created our own heaven, let me die for it. Truly love in some faraway heaven does hang a hammock. We water our youths by our muse, as ill-tempered men show not a hotter fire than a poet's spirit's rage. A love for a beauty inspired, but unfound in life. Only in wonderous fantasy, between reality and inner strife. But die, soul. For it is my hurt and pain; dying in the end on a mission in life to conquer a world dead the same. Take care in thy muse, for one overwatered cannot cherish a lover's clinging roots.

Oh rose, you hold droplets of full naked despair, but I am emptied by the moonlit sky, your beautiful silken hair. You shined like this melody so long ago, and empty thoughts I hold are still naked and pain ridden in my love I once knew so rare. Now I wake to this somber voice alone. But rest is in thee. If I could have loved thy sweet sounds, so shall my peace be. But light and flowers hold not hope to one hiding, hidden from all whose faulty eye may see. The birth is the last thing we think of resurrecting, but it is that death that makes us live more happy. Without your tone, my ears deafen to wake. And sight for thee, oh! still I keep. My wish takes my laughter throughout the fields of yellow flowers, but wrecks myself in the flattering rot of a wailing hour. This death I've written means nothing. It fuses all, poisoning our flower, the one we held together; the thing that barely lets me live in this cold weather. I am the payee of your debts, and shall live to love, never.

Can this soul love you away when finding past my faults for space for true love to rent? When I lack for vehemency, thou must temperament. Any other eyes may be blessed that discover the pacific waters of thy soul, far too rich to comprehend. Like a river, you swoon past any lands end, to cut your beauty's swath on all eyes of man. You enliven these dry fields and raise enough harvest to sacrifice enough self for reasons of the wind. Once I lacked any heart or sin. Fly, for in this wind we can only blow away, knowing not where we've come or where we'll stay. But unto love sweetly I wrap woven garnets atop that body most beauteous below your celestial face. But miss me when I'm gone, and I shall cry too, for I've only lived to love in scorn. The phantom I pray to for an answer one day. A girl's eyes summoned in life does still lack. Free as a winged jest, my love always unto thee, poetry, shall always come back.

This soul, not worth the land it has bought. I try to find some love in skin, but all in despair and entirely in rot. So I dare not expand my wealth I've already emptied, till a lover's eyes excuse their excuses and share their inner riches, instead of their time for monetary value on which they dwell. To find what it is inside my lover's eye with truth in my muse, for they are all words unshared and greedy lines fooled. The patience of my love depends on you. The way I touch her still is ghostly felt. But she loves my rhyme, and the sensation in her unknowingly times. Vengeance has passed my love by. But now in shadow I have told her my diligent sigh. So fear not these words unto you I can find. My love fears the lack of caress in my soul so ripe, yet tricked unwell. I part not with love, yet the sky for now lacks some angel above.

Love, I cannot write to you anymore. Impassionate and in desperation, I have lost my muse. And if my moon says it so, might it be with you? I have heard of hard times being in this state of mind I am. But you are an angel. In serpent condescendence I pray to change more like a human again. Where is my fate, but in the crowned king whose judging eye shall have me sent unto his labyrinth? I wish upon this muse that stars could find my love, this power that grips my soul all alive for her eyes. And my lust, a tortured vacation searching her for sensation. The hot sun, a still earth, and a quiet soul still make my roads dark. But I shall find what sad mirrors reflect when after you have passed, how inspiration can rekindle in this man. It is love, oh dear fate, that I, humble though in past regret, give my soul that has searched sore and lumbering, shall now be able to satiate. And angel or not, I can find my peace in some nymph who will quell my humming and steal slow my soul still searching instead of being so wretchedly bought. I will hold onto thee as long as I may, but withered, weak, and woe, I fear through time travelled gone we'll tumble away in the wind blown.

My love is but dead. The only way I find you now, is this rhyme in my head. You looked so sweet, dashing before my eyes in a dream; now so soon I am within to bleed. What is my heart now, but a black unamorous plow, harvesting death that was sown and planted with a kiss and touch, and presently adorned with a dark gaping gesture – a hellish false love unannounced. But I need not words to display my love for thee. Too many times we've danced. And I perish the thought of uncovering hell once again. Live on muse, but find a way to determine hell's end.

Why am I so mad? I felt as if I could live to love all, but still within I am poignantly sad. Death is but my shiver, your cold hand. I wish that we would have loved, but instead now I am ruined as I walk upon all of my empty land. Even if the gloom overwhelms this love of mine, its sweetness I wish could have been had. I phrase the sorrow of a thoughtful rose I knew we both held, yet only I was left to remain eternally alone and merrily sad. If only life replayed its verse, and parts played in our time took sides with love's infinite words. Now only in my lone heart always terse, for our love did not exist. I am mad unto myself – my own curse. It lurked alone in grateful rhyme and in wonderful verse.

At last I can see my love alone, for as I waste my longing youth, the hand of time dearly I see has taken you for exchange of love all its own. I will not rest now, for this high battle shall be won. If it be not for thee, then for that love once had now gone. Life without you is but despair in a long discourse, and love unexisting only in my heart while it fades. My distance prevents me from sharing my rhythm with love. Perhaps time, who stole my beauty's hand, shall not seal doom, but now reap creation of a new love I protect as I water her bloom. Oh, love shall destroy time's ends and save me from death; alack, I have not loved. And kill me too soon in no love, to have not even lived.

If only my own hands could touch what my dreams could see, then my dreams are real, no longer fantasy. Love is dark wherever eyes lurk. Only death between life and love does search. The matter of life exists not, only love in a word. The only way a dream is real is silent, an inner realm, slowly becoming an inside hell. Only an angel's wing can be severed before you realize the fallen have been there, and know it too well. Death plays a part in dreams and breaks life's dark glass so shattering. The heart and all dreams become our world – better than reality? Fantasy's hands can weave all they can while rage of love spews forth at the accosted dream of lovers to be, in dreams only had. Fantasy plays life as doom comes passing by, and in dreams, a muse is found wretched and huddling sad at night. Destroyed by lover's dreams and all hope of love alive.

1/20/99

I am crushed by the landslide of your beauty. Ripples in this pristine water of your soul reflect the love I feel so deep and moving. It gives me pause, since I am at the will of your ways always soothing. Test me and I cannot say a word. Only love can I show to thee arousing. Only bliss of love is my exit, and I, disdainful of your pretty face, find myself all for doom inside. In past hells, all in unhealth erase. So wondrous is your whim, that when painting what you have carved in my soul, it cannot compare to thee. I match only too dim. Murderous of my own soul I become inside me. I wish feelings for thy beauty could be less preposterous and more free. To join its essence in the soul's balance, to finally be.

Oh painful love, you wreck my eyes and heart. You make a constant struggle for my life, and dearest sadden me together, and wretchedly when we part. Never was I victim to your hands. She somewhere blooms the flower I gave, but now sadly, sickly, I rest on thorns burning up this body in a terrible land. My love could touch your body, to mold from your clay-like substance a rhythm of pleasure on your persuasive tan. What lies forward from this melody, but bliss of your love on the beaches of heaven's sands. The girl that gave me life still breathes in to me, and I return thy love so free. But alone I am in loving words to thee. My heart is painful, as always. Death is only a somber pardon to those souls seeking a dead retribution, faking eyes to darkness where we all shall leave.

Through pain endured, the love I swirl, and the hell I roam, it becomes a dying girl. Why is my hell in love? That now I am haunted by a beauty now far gone, still foreboding over my lone trail, a dark sky. A moon eclipsed by a sun at night. Love shall not prevail. Will rest come someday when I am alive, or when I die? The rest of life cowers before me, but by my befitted powers it does not love like so sweetly to thee. Heaven's glance is a window to tomorrow, and yesterday is a devilish night; a burning darkness heading forth past all eyes, to blinding light. Dead trees cut a valley in two, and my sight over these tired hills begins to count on love so true. If only my passion could equal my desire, and then possession would rule out my fire. The rose stands still. And my soul rests here. The grave is gone, but still my dead love does dig. My love for you, Kim... you must realize my eternal wrath of life I live. Only as I die to rest, die to live, live too fast, live to die, live to find my way, darkened by a kiss; the kiss of pain, and a glance. A cunning saga of classical love, a poignant boy, cursed by gothic romance. Kim, love never was meant like this to stay attached. So find me sweetest in thy dark heart, and let me pray before I disavow all faith to thee, myself, and god. I shall break away soon, if you do indeed part. Thank you love, I've found my treasure sought.

Free of injustice and might of my shrine, a being is closer to their spirit and safer in the vast depths of all respected time. To remain a part of the great feud, one can find memories past but not left behind. And life colored in mystery shows what you've always wanted to know to the time aligned. Find a part of yourself that no other being can sense to be felt. Touch that other side with care, and deal with life in the realm which it has been weld. No one else has this many grains to sift even if the wind does go adrift. With each grain a gift; hope and memories of the best days on earth left to live.

A glass pane hovers above in direct light of the sun. Trees outside hang about scratching on the pane; dead wood by a quiet church alone. A high ceiling by a large door loom within the dark, and from the center of the sacred ground, eyes at broadest see carvings on the walls that encircle torches burning slow and long. Perches float high, intertwined on the old ceiling where two crows in silence sing a toneless song. Black feathers fall and collect on the felt ground, while the winds force through fissures of the tightly built stone walls. When a last candle lights upon the altar, the rest become dim as the shadow of night shines down the smoke colored glass; a narrow ray of moon filling a piece of darkness frightened by a placid light unmoved. The tome under the ripped silk is uncovered, and the small bell above rings out loud and long. Happiness here is home under the dim light surrounded by nothingness and no one at all. The stained glass tingles with light when the crows dip their heads silent at dawn, like the first time I found this place in the midnight rain, full of roses so long ago.

When the bleak weather takes its toll on my body, the freezing jets my blood to somewhere warm, far from me. In these cold environs, the caverns chill my spine, yet at home I am here with nothing to follow my lead. These still, dark halls lighted by candle every night with curtains in an inanimate chamber not replaced for a century, wreath a clock gathering webs never looked upon, but always right. Time counts for sleep during the light, and leaving these still walls to wander about in danger of dawn keeps the hidden awake at wondrous night. With a smile tugging at the corners of his mouth, the black shrouded pale traveler randomly casts his looks upon his victim's eyes. With merciless fury, ten fall before him, and the killer feeds before daylight. The light fades and shadows feed his eternal and dreaded soul. At rest once again, this cavernous home becomes his coffin. For many untold years amongst mortal men, in silence he waits to banish blood in dark dreams of the end.

By the daylight hour, while resting alone in a bleak unadorned chamber, I see the sky full of the darkest weather. The sun hides behind the clouds, behind these dreamy lines, and how cold it is alone in these fleeting confines. A solitary flower creeps across the window where it glows, perhaps to be happier than the day's weather assigned. Trapped within a sad spirit, petals fall like a cape drenched in the rain before some morbid duel. By the little rays of light shining in the dark window, it feels like a place to find an otherworldly portal. But I miss the world, to adapt to everything new. I sought its love but came out undead before a cross knelt, pale and doomed. I see the petals spread forth on the glass; its infinite compassions still compare to the night's black rain. I reach out, so to crush the flower, and rid its pain. I dash out of this high tower with a breaking dark window, and I am free.

Atop of my life in a sky so blue yet full of dark clouds, I exist plainly in a wretched storm in the midst of hell. Some black wind howling as my push of lust holds evil so beautifully well. In pain, my sacrifices are met. The giving blood I poured out over those high dark hills of life never by thee love, were gingerly wept. And blank stupidity draws out before my eyes, and life becomes colorless. And I, hopeless unto sorrow, wear a naked yet dark disguise. The only way that I can live is to push out this pain of lust, my sad state, to only in disgust watch the collecting scars from advancing age on the skin of beauty once young, now dead to the eye's taste. Love touches the past of a now darkened mind. There was beauty in their faces, even in tired lies, not recent parting after parting, nor faint song in the duel of hated love. My blackest trophy – a journey led too long to live a normal life. I cross myself as high as I've gone, since now I realize only to love I've cried too long. Simple dreams haunt this spell of life and wreck a soul immersed in questioning dead love; a black wind to themselves be petrified.

In a kiss of dreamy love, my fantasies yearn for her, to make her my only tone. The past is a graveyard of dead wishes unfelt among my words I feel so. If only desire lit the great hellish fire of yearning alone in this dark tower, I would be in the sun touching the beauty of you - that sweet, tender flower. An excited world depends on what visions I can see of thee, though I, heartless and lacking power, gloomily stare from afar. All hopes and dreams at the same time pour endlessly, yet still alone in this magical hour. I rest the days away quietly still. But this chamber becomes my youth, and wishing it and I could touch your much younger love, withdraws my hope even more.

Searching far within, a dark angel struggles with chains my emotions have tangled her pale body in. I leave her cold and desirous of living again, just as she did when the sunshine of life for me began. Hellish, so far in my soul; this wretched demon proudly took my love, and an entire youth did it steal. Yet, alone inside in the dark rain on cold nights she cries out to be free. But never can my heart be loving, so full of light to shine upon her desperate plea. Since in depths beneath all happiness, all worth living, she has made invisible my spirit; empty. A lost realm outside a window of colored glass reflects images brought to life by the creature of an unkind past. Wind unlatches these locks, and down the colors runs the reality of time – touching tears flowing, falling on the dark dwindling angel inside. The chains are gone, and she flies far away to a fading love the same as mine. Still by this window I hear fantasies cry; searching dreams of living, but finding only blackness inside. As clouds part to form the blue sky, love, flying high, is that dark angel always wanting to cry, but still it remains the most precious to life.

Tones kept long and low quell my heart to think that life holds more love for me to adore, while gazing upon a light in the midst of constant darkness which this earth becomes without sight of thee. As eyes in love harp on the hells of my restrained tone, why does thy face fade so fast in loved memory? Or that your sweet ways must dim in my thoughts caved in by the sharp granite of thine eye still searching? Our hearts slowly do fade, while quick time speeds our youth passing many a masquerade. Your love to awake takes my spirit past its full ripeness to see that the fruit of thy being and soul has planted itself not to be admired in grace, but blossomed full for the season of one lover's taste. Two dueling tones in the rain circle each other's opposite pain of love, but fighting for the same beauty's face in some way unto themselves alone. Words defeat them both, as the somber beauty runs away cold. They fight honorably forever, their clash of blades becoming my song. Writing to you, love, is but a bliss found in tone. My sad spirit jauntingly awakes to thee, for new love is but an unpicked fruit alone, digested not to the desire of love's hunger, but to the taste of its freshness; for eyes that shine upon thee never again must need to roam.

At the summit of my pleasure, or any of my pain, there lies a beauty without answers, I suffer to blame. The creator of my heart and killer of all my love; she strikes my soul for eternity, since she was the first of all. Desperate at such horrible hours, fate is this demon haunting me. And now my sadness turns to a hurting grey just as new love in my small garden begins to flower before the sun today. For so long has my hell reproached my pace, and thy hallowed tears worsen this, remarrying another love, making my sighs for thee diligent in replace. Oh why must vengeance take place in the very heart within whose love at a time shared with thee cries now unpeaceful, yet free. To cross you meant my bitter end, but still in the cold rain my spirit finds you heavenly again. But now that you're gone, all I am is a passion compiled for pain. Oh, I blame thee naught for these tricked senses! My heart is the one to blame.

I've fed the images of long ago, but write to a phantom cradled in my arms now. Safe from the haunted picture painted as I walk the past, from time to time I dare to go. Love, you are never of a season, nor any muse. Yet you plague me with tricks and remorse at the very blossom of spring, and under the bright stars where giant Taurus looms. I am unfree to live, so long as these chains I still must grapple with as a bard. Dire relief is sad eloquence for a beauty who fades distant over life's ever-changing sparse marsh. With no recompense, but pure disdain, roots in my inner land cannot water thine or mine own heart, so my somber tone stays the same. Words faintly fog from a voice, one whose soul is half in the sun, half in the rain; a lone, shambled, gray figure, embittered by years of intolerable feign. A child is held coldly wrapped in words, sleeping at night through the trials of sorrow in the master's eye-sinking and swooning world steeped in pain. This broodling becomes myself; all present thoughts harbored by the past unwell. Love is the only to survive, yet dead to tell. So the picture of her beauty sinks into that phantom fed in my soul, dictating all my hours and crying; needing one goodbye from her over that horizon on our now desolate hill. And when I am old, I cradle my memory, as the phantom takes me a last time over the flowers, into the darkness at will.

Inner Strife   3/19/99

Pain is the facet for my suffering; a place to hide inside this difficult
soul, with meanings of love that yet cannot be paused by constant
deciphering alone. By my heart I do not see thee, for words unto
myself create a blank melancholy. Tones do not flow as beautifully
as long ago, and my hate for love shows that it has never been
known. It can be longing that makes a stormy mind wander outside
in the rain, where thoughts of the past bring to life inner strife as
creativity takes away the pain. The overwhelming emotion makes
beauty within die quick stricken in pain, and all the masses of
thoughts worthy of life find death in your name. And without some
love or hope I wish to have or have been, I struggle but cannot give.
But this shall be the end. Dying slow, poetry, thou hath been my
saddest friend.

At the beginning of life there exists no time; a place of joy colliding with the spirits of the outer realm, creating rhyme. But so possessed of unearthly matter, one should rid themselves of an unblessed line, through the eye of others; to them a dubious sign. For love I write, but constant trial against all sense of this sprouts from a sad image, this thing unpleasantly, yet heavenly alive. A hope that some dream or a rare thought of love within could wreck my soul into thinking that truly my existence bases itself on the hells of a faded love, somber, so sweet to my eye. My possession is forced into making loving souls slumber as these devils plead for me to arrive... my sense is blinded by a passion to go on with life – to fit within rules that overstay my very power to write. For this, proof comes with the end of any of our lives, which reveals no spectre – not one soul expelled true to our time. And so in quest, the end is bitter by better life once lived, in silence so we fight.

Forever clouds eternity's perception, and my mind now leaks forward to one of these directions. Somewhere in my mind the past comes to life, for this soul finds present reason for insurrection; to rid myself of some happy future to delay an ancient memory's resurrection. Mention love, and all my heart goes into it. Therefore a needful religion shall take its place in this image. Late nights hallowed by a quiet and cold alone, call for the demons of old; a glimpse at a time my far innocent flesh could not contain these now distant and hated, yet loved souls. I cannot forgive nor forget, and so my mind stained by the past is shattered by indigenous regret. Memories! ...the cause of all of this. An erasure of all these held whims I do indeed try to dismiss, for love means love only by a simple kiss.

The thorns of feelings spawned by the past long ago bring wrath upon me, as the broadest feeling crying on forever comes within its way to be seen. I forget myself amongst the fields of wildflowers – and her – over the high bog reeves across the low, quiet, and bubbling blue stream, I make haste for a bridge to feast eyes on what closer inspection may reveal of thee. But unnoticed and gone, she entices me still to write on. To look and search shall bring no answer, only a vision of hair blowing in the wind, blonde. But I close my eyes and reopen them again, and there she stands still with several poppies in hand. The bridge cannot exist, nor does the plains, girl, or a giving land, but pure despair for a force not half as great as the real scene had. Hair in the wind blows to grey, and a bubbling river is an overflowing swamp today. The sky is red, and her face a shadow, fleeing from flowers now all thorned, forcing beauty to match pain. All that remains is a dark spectacle, a wasteland I stand in still. And to all that come here, they know, that a beautiful scene is plucked by a deceitful girl. And it is where you learn: beauty in its blossoming hour is not to love forever as it's sworn, for this rose will not be picked unto love, no. Blood will drip in woe from the beauty and pains of love's thorns.

Trying to make my words worth double their nature, to make them more rare, I only remember still how much you did not worry, how you did not even jokingly care. I see those roses in hand, day after day by sweat and rain and love in his deed, that boy who sought to deliver the gifts immortal still within me. Something earthly, innocent, and rare, picked in the purest of goodness; flowering petals to give to her I dared. Perhaps she did not see them, or saw too late, but still precious thoughts wane into older age, sifting a memory that blooms waterless in times struggle, infinite fate. Her ways I never found. I only waited for a dream to fill the reality I could have never known. I wish her angel guided her to my truth; for the stars no longer gleam, and for what is writing, what is life, without this dark scene... I remember only her always, and never more I ever received. I stubbornly search for something that would not be. Death in life so young created by longing's sight, sorrowfully ends any hope of dreams in tender love outright.

Lucky I am to find a paper on which to write. What is more than all these rhymes, all these once breathing incarnations kept inside? Life is keeping my eyes open, treasures aside, to only watch for her, even if my true love faded in time finds in her that I am a lie. In quietude I am in a new life, even in a new love's eyes. My actions, generous though they may be, as the harvest begets the seed, ruin a past gentle hearted, fragrant with melody. To hold the notes one more line would kill the last. Tones frozen forever locked inside. Sounds of yesterday fertile within, yet scorn and pale the present to reap. To see my matter is oblivious, knowing a bird will not sing, and I can see not for I tire of man; his blind curiosity sought. Thoughts like these end so simple in time. Thoughts of the end encompass my dream; this love I've held so long inside. I deny my fate, deny character, and for all my life I hold my love so dear, yet never will I serenade her. Passion in me dwells not in life to confide. Love for her is a long, dead rhyme. And unlucky I am, for the end is what I write.

A Last Thought of You   6/2/99

I wrote an end first, the summer does to my pen call. My spirit
undelighted by love, the thing I cannot believe many men have
found, yet I do not receive in beckoning call. My luck seems to me
to be at fault; only once to the dark day for did emotion with spirit
rise. Past, newer youth, my wonder imbued to her, unto beauty's
eyes. A secret kept, wept in hope. Then came the dawn, to let every
man know what dreams and hell she created in my soul. I wish in
myself if it be not for my past beauty, cherished love, then to future
encounters of falling eyes, some girls knowing in the soul exactly
what goes on. To end with you has been a chamber in hell, but
beauty inside that wonderfully matches my life's song. Steps to fate
creek two feet feeling why does it matter how life is always tried to
be lived so long, and hoping my life could have been better filled by
a reality of love. With head rested still, my spirit: regretted guilt.
Knowing I cannot live to see a child after the slow blade falls above.
Though I will make years more of grief, perhaps a better life to live
to see only another death alone. Unknown in approach, the reaper
speaks... and the final words give to me strength. But only now still
does a lingering thought of you set my spirit at ease.

From that first dawn I sat writing in the grass above the stream, a melody soft and poignant in rhythm above the bog reeves. Where it would take me, I did not yet know. Holes in the leaves shined in bits of sun. First I was this and alone, then found by beauty, a beauty alone; seemingly this and nothing more. She turned me into a spell, one whose sleep wept for love, and sad when awake. A twinge of misery given to me, accepted in fated pain forced once on me by her upon, then to all souls I could condone. But those leaves painted in my rhythm, undying love for some oddity in my heart. A false, yet giving totem erected to her forever on that day forward did my answer come to falter, yet did it start, that some cosmic love infinite in its muse came to me in loving say; yet still to me unreal – a vision untrue. My question only was where the soul shall go... the gardens of Greece, Egypt, a temple of Rome – now I know. Life becomes of our only death with a long hymn to initiate that song. But love awoke long ago, and perhaps not even so, these crows no longer would know what it means to me, how nature unto life makes love unfold.

Arcane knowledge comes at night, stalking thoughts spirited yet with fright. If love continues, I will become one of its singing slaves, therefore I cannot show what my youth wishes with my plight. I am slain by the coldness of my rhyme, and burning of love. Power is taken and never given, so I consent to the pain of my loss. But my lady, the one in this storm of a mind, why must you dearly plague by day and haunt by night? For dreams are dearer than thy untouched form, so dearer than pleasant sight. The victim I am by accepting your love; these conscious dreams wanted long. My muse has tolerated ills of love overwrought with quickening of my soul to a death with her, now knowingly wrong. In her arms I was rotted and forgotten by time. Whose foul deeds diced my character by a mad sickle, a crooked knife; his hideous ways aside. Beauty will go back to nothing, from whence she came. I will remain here longer, longer the same.

It is the old who breed despair amongst the young. Witches become of girls as they grow young to old, in silence for an entire life to rule the world as man rules abroad. Hell does reach a peak, when anger that breathes in the past explodes in the present when a cluttered soul silently weeps. The olden war begins again, for each day that passes adds to the bitterness of man. A somber light imprudent to the passions of other's cries, shining in on the dead, whose foul means stay alive in these old ones lacking wise thoughts, and malignancy and taintedness about their souls beside. Oh woe, turmoil lies in me, since I know living too old is past the limits of our youths, and the only true goodness in this world is time's forgetfulness... youthfulness and its fruits. Where old bones make quick death seem a century long, they make new skin terrified by old life in a thousand forms been, now gone all wrong. As a youth I stand ready to fall amongst an ever-advancing world. Advancing thicker I try to grow some mental shell. To corrupt this world by knowing little, only time well, old ones steal youth though they've known it once themselves. As they breathe my despair ruins life. But old souls know better; better to live than to die, to see what was built in the past far from their time to further mankind.

I have long thought that I would lose a gift given, ages away, now empty tone. Past conclusions I finish in this future, remembering only one to this day, unseen long ago. And as wretches tear my esteem, I am plagued by a greater remorse, greater than love's great deed. If the sun could burn into love, let it be more than this somber glow in tone. The sky resides ethereal, atop the mind; but to lay by thee, if even I see again true love, it is a constant goodbye. Yet by your very empty hole inside, contained within a sigh, seconds break down to hours, slowing the soul I am inside. All fear what they have created within; a malfunction in the machine, attacking the creator as gods become slaves. I lose the gift given over time in the wind and rust of rhyme. The heart that beats in man is so many of a trivial tone. Where uncovered in love, there creates that undying fashionable glow. Found in hate, which destroys your character, to destroy your all. And in the vast world with most, they are best left alone.

All I feel is the constant death in everyone's mind. I am sad, for I know it is a sick habit they carry, embedded in instinct; yet you fool, thou canst keep it inside. They think me a corpse, to plot to take a soul already died. Even when alive, it is a sad joke to steal from the dead. Either intelligent and evil, or stupid and good, everyone works alone to improve themselves, for it is a race for the perfect god. This weight I carry means nothing anymore. For I hold the silence inside and now you have nothing to hate at all... Ha, ha, ha, ha. Sick of these humans, who think their lives could take another, whose souls are truly as wrecked as each other. The creative force in any life creates our good. Your evil, or any other, is thy lack of temperance and character; too much love, or a stupid mind as blind as the dark. The intelligible power grants influence on another, at whose face I will never again look upon. Control is given only to the self. Abuse and breed it past that, then I think you should be kept to some kind of private hell. For in this race to death we cannot outrun one another. For god lies not in you or me, though you think he does, but fate's deadly hour. Change is the most important to life. And wherefore if thy dreams, love, or thy soul is tried to be stolen, beware. Be against the blind gods in man, the ones in the past who've slain the hour at hand, since they think they're right. Fight alas in hope at least amongst these foolish, dark individuals in life, to try to keep thy freedom free; to see thy precious sight.

Myself. A tragedy; dreams unfelt. Love unknown, unreal, unheld.
Hate. No opposite to anything; just what you feel for me. Justice. It
hides unrest. No one loves a perfect soul, left to only be killed by
one faraway and alone. Sleep. So close to death; without it, you
cannot finish this test. Fear. The thing you implant in me. I drive it
only headfirst, and my body takes the punishment. Listen. You will
hear your blank voice in others. Silent at first, and louder as they
pin you to their own evil. Hell. The only thing universal, since you
try to examine me. Love once more, two kinds. Something that
without adoration, wrecks this life and makes your death that very
object. Pain, pleasure, unlearn doubt. See life in yourself, only there,
never in others. Intrusion contains the death. The thing between,
for there must be a master to everything. Tears. An undying, yet
broken communication intercepted. Mind. Without it, you are bliss.
Death is something close to it. Time. Simply a place where all others
in this reality insist upon having you fit.

I write on the opposite side of my constant curse; love always indifferent, so I hate everything including myself. I look everywhere, even in the moon... where she may look? I cannot see any dream, for love or lust pains my death as it takes hold. I rest in myself; feel terrible within. A beauty for my cry, for what is life's worth without your fate wanted, knowing that you in bravery could have, but so dearly so paranoid 'til the end. The beauty in this, in her - though I know love is not universal. Feign death, for I am weak. And love is a cruel maze, a labyrinth I devise to block my very own faith. A faith for her, but why? She will not show the love like in my eyes, and you continue to weaken me, and now I am paralyzed. The nail driven by mercy, who knows that only by mine or your bleeding, will love truly have any affection for me. O truly man is a cursed soul. Blemished in dreams wanted with her; if you cannot, you stay trapped inside beauty. But then truly, beauty is always alone. Without a way, flowers rot, and in this will I delve deeper into my own soul; to become vicious within, and spend prayer in hell. Life deals me a jagged, twisted, unhad, and terrible wished for love, that will shine on the outside never more. I seal myself up, and all I have now is a blasphemous cage, in macabre despair, so I roam. Justification between lust and love is time's fault, for I sit beside no one, and only in myself can this creature be called she; for it is passion in me, resolute or not, I cannot solve.

You encircle my ways. My center above all is my own unrest these days. I seek myself, finding in you. But I know the between is dangerous to everything. To heal my mind, to patch up this disaster, what in future years to come, I feel my life flowing in and out, faster. There is a dead mind, but a living spirit behind all of this. How could I, being so gloom, understand how this all unfolds? Yet I hold back, taunting my own whim. Fools people are to fear themselves, and not understand. This is the way retribution could end. For the soul strikes wrath, and I am plagued within.

Change inside, forever changing within. There comes a time when all losses become our gain. To look back to when friends, the ones that have perished long ago, appear before our eyes once again to remember far away times. To shift back to a beautiful scene in life, to share our loved memories with those that have died. You gave me power. Knowledge unknown until you came along. I learned a new way of life. But now, I do not know where you have gone. I miss our talks we once had; about the girl I loved, how she left me alone and sad – a confused young boy's fate. How we chanted on about obsolete models of processors all too soon to be out of date. There were tremors within you - painful reminders of the past, and its debt. But still, you wheeled along through life like a man free of all pain, and any regret. Deep inside, it was terrible that the world did you wrong. So I walk down the same paths we took, thinking of my life now, where it goes I still can't control. Osiris, goodbye friend. I will remember your struggle, and all I learned from you in the end – and the reinforcement, a beckoning hand. An inspiration you gave to me: as a man thinketh, so shall he.

Rain into Silence   11/29/01

I dream alone this day. Remembering my love, the thing I could not
have – she called to me from afar, and as I raised myself to talk, all I
wanted was to hold her in my arms. Life has gone by quicker than
any of us would think. Without, the days pass as if they were a leaf
down a shallow stream. But time has its moment; a moment of
silence, a meaningless glance. To look into the future, yet all I can
do is hold on to the past. To yearn, to dream again. In disheartening
truth, all I can do is make ink flow from the end of a pen. I reach
into a space I have seen and known for many long years where I
have pondered, praying for the wind to shift, thus, bringing you
back. And as the rain falls outside ever so light, all I remember are
the enchanted days; lost dreams of her residing in my past. But my
doubts make my fear. The cold winter will consume all I wish. My
dream will never be real, as long as I exist.

                                                        12/3/01

Sleep – it never ends. I look for a girl somewhere within, and I am
alone again. The only one I loved departs my heart, and to dream
alone is the pity I suffer for never loving that which was loved.
Alone we both are now, and I suffer within. I search and search, but
never to find one like her... the first to touch my heart the way she
did. All I can do is remain in sorrow, for I never woke up from this
dream to see reality – what love we could have had.

Under the Tree   12/8/01

To write to you once again takes me where I wish I had been; under the tree alone with her. Under the tree we could talk of life, whatever we felt about us. I remember when I felt true love only for you. I feel the same way still. I thought you'd forget all my wrongs and come back again. Under the tree I wait for her in what seems like eternal shade, as night becomes a new day, to undo all my misdoings and make each other feel the way we did. But now after long years that pass us by, under that tree thinking of you all this time, I can still see carved in the bark, a T and K, surrounded by a heart. But regret makes me feel like she's forever gone. I wanted to love you, but fate did us wrong. Under the tree I sit, and dream alone.

When the wind climbs, breathing against my back, I turn around to only see her cry in the midst of the rain in the dense fog on a dark, chilling night. To watch her fade into the shadows she was born from, to disappear as mysteriously as she came. Rain drips from the end of my fingers as I reach out to touch the apparition of this dream. Her veils, white as snow; her eyes a beautiful green, yet to look into them strikes my very soul. In a somber gaze, both green marbles orbiting, floating, within her ghostly skull. I fall to my knees, begging the rain to stop my horrid dream, as the image begins to twist and shudder, as if it were cold in this dark downpour of heaven's tearful waste. I see her old stare upon her face; the one I remember there from so long ago - a face that within my mind, I could never erase. The fog dissipates around her, and as she walks away, fading into the mist from whence she came, I feel she has taken her toll. A debt for many years I have not paid – something I regret? It was merely a ghost, what could I say? She takes my undying love for her back to the grave - my love being a martyr to this day, unknown to us when we both were alive… a thing I could never confide. Into the rain-filled night she withers, and long years thereafter, so shall I. We are not a memory, but a kind of love unkind to us, that echoes, plaguing man through the ages, where countless souls feel these things inside. A cemetery of dreams where men bury their hopes of love for all time.

The infection spreads within. Blood rippling through our veins, a pox to destroy the soul; to steal it before it can escape past the unknown. A trophy, made of dust collected inside, where dreams of love become dead over time. Disease and sickness strike the core of my body, and peel away at my humanity. Doomed to fall while the putrid worm travels up my spine, I merely fake a death, one at a time. Who will be next, no one knows - this curse, the soul infection – more hideous than any death known. Bloody blisters form from within. Bulging red sores eating away at my skin. Two tumors high to low, corrupting everything earthly that I own as my body begins its fall. Carving out of my innards, piercing and eviscerating my flesh – a grim reminder rears its head. Fed on the last of my soul, this monster rises from my chest. Absorbed with my blood it now begins to crow and claw, ripping away the last of what remains of my torso. Slowly I rot into oblivion; my skin with a pallid tint changing to a green-gray. The creature I bore leaps out of this body to find its prey. To stalk and fester like a new plague, and wreck havoc on all of humanity in its way. The last drops of blood within me it takes as some kind of morbid trophy. "Who will inherit this lad's death?" The gravedigger sings, as he piles dirt over my wretched corpse, now just a hollow body. And so, I am buried alongside the rest of the dead. To wait for rebirth, so I can feed from their souls once again...

I could own everything I've ever wanted, pray to a god invisible, with an unanswered quandary. But never adjoin a love I've hidden for years. A love I've sought from within – haunted. Life flows deep in vast rivers flowing into eternity, as Charon's raft drifts below on the Styx under us encircling. Hopeless without the thing I seek, to rule the world while millions soft in silence sleep. Remembering my love never had, but only in this dream now awoken by a flame that engulfs the very core of me. A dark flame I cannot touch, nor see. The flames bring a lost love forgotten, back to torture my memory. All I am, all I own is nothing in the end. Only my dear love I search fruitlessly for within. To plague my days on this earth as a man, to steal my soul and die one day; as many times as I already have. But never in my wildest dreams will I ever love a beauty like you again...

To sting them as I've been stung. A solo warrior guiding blade into bone. To vanquish my memory, creating havoc sharper than my foe's tongue. The demon to be slain: mere words too weak to say. An axe prepared, fading away in bloody haze, all my thoughts that the demon awakes. For every fool known as 'she' has made her way, all killed by dealing doom to end my pain. A revenant, galloping and charging into glorious battle, with a rage that cannot be healed. A gash bloodied by disgust and reckless wake. These creatures never are worth what men embrace, but deceive as willingly as my whirling blade. So I plunge into blood-soaked battle, that their memory may fade, and let rage take over as I fell my foes and forget them amongst the corpses of the slain. A bloodied spear of woe impaling everyone as they approach. To win this fight though it never ends, oh let me as strong as my armored plate, forget, obliterate, and slay this cursed memory and future trials of female demons blocking and chiding the way. When all enemies have been killed to appease my vengeance and hate - suppressing instincts, but obeying my rage, as I stand upon piles of their remains, defying this noble warrior has put them in their place.

Now a slow fall into my depths, turning more a monster every day, with self control being wrest in an inner realm of pain. I cannot live on whilst the world, as full of fools as it may be, are joyful in their dreams; yet I am chiding my soul, torturing sanity. Banishing interlopers, and indulging in wrath upon the end. Taking years inside still never fulfilled within; a hunger or need constantly tamed. A monster born of hate, an uncaring soul once kind in all ways now wishing to kill all love, forcing all femininity to the flames. Tortured and malignant, rotting from dire instincts - a beast within I kill over and over to satiate my unfed whim. There its corpse lies, and I wait for it to rise again. Ripping my spirit, staining me, with torturous pain that no man should withstand alone in this cold world where I become the same; an echo of wretched instinct of these desires I so hate – a beast unto myself, chained within; a raging scorn with an unbeguiled interest once aflame. I bury these now dead emotions, thousands of corpses hidden away, with no fight appearing to exist; but inside, a grim factory designed to quiet the horrors of yearning so long within. Destructing love, and all sense of character, as a spirited beast slowly dying; wishing my heart would simply quit its march, for unto this battle I lose - could only hope to meet my fate. That I may die and enter the next, I need not worry or pretend. A battle-torn monster now, all my years I spend. Tiring of being the empty beast in this singular life; I wish it to end. And unto this world I will avoid, never to return again.

God is here. God is great. God is everything we create. God is good, God is now; in every humble bow.

God is splendor, grand; the cosmic wheel – a divine plan.

It supports our shelter: God provides though we roam alone. In catastrophe and utopic illusions where no crosses are borne by our whimsical flesh – a threshold the human race sadly shall never reach nor behold.

God is dear, yours and mine. Close yet far, in our hearts for years to come. A trust as if unto family, or our sacred home.

God is light. For we shed our luminescence to experience its world as our own; venturing out from wisdom, and all arcane heights. Tasting the fruit, and discovering creation, and man and wife.

Our body is our tower; the temple to our dear lord. And as I lie down to touch rejuvenation of my mortal flesh in sleep, gently pulling down a stream in time flowing away, I shall remember I am here to face the test of will. Knowledge already known, discipline now needs to be shown.

God, forgive me of my ruin within, but bless those for caring. For this cross I bear is not the first nor last humans shall see. When I am void and alone one day, hoist me up when I am full of luster and unempty.

God is the kingdom of my soul; vast uncharted land, isles untold.

God is within, and I am proud to be loved so bold.

And when death for me come, on some day the world nor any spirits may not mourn, somber yet unchained – free of a husk, flying within infinite waves of vast seas. A universe we already now could know.

At last, pure soul. I shall remember my beautiful mortal form. So long as the wheel spins and I am of intangible whole, may God let me to dream and pray for all life in centuries to come, and return to the world and be with the one love we all wish we had that I felt so long ago.

This body is the kingdom of my soul - vast spirit bearing weighted pain from heights untold. Higher ascended strength within recreates wrath of searing pain on skin. Raw and acrid, beaten and withered flesh. I remain staunch and spirited until the end, as nothing more supports the weight of a thousand crosses. Mud into dirt to sand from dust unto ashes I've been, from all the sticks and stones piled atop corporeal hands. A passionate phoenix burning inside, into the kingdom wrought with tools of doom no longer standing aside. Harmony – theirs and mine. Now I into a reincarnate find. To be that liberated soul an entire world for eternity could deeply confide, as now ashen bone becomes flesh though seared by the stains of scourged mortal men. Their leaders in false triumph stand. One must spite their folly, for every being reaches an end no matter their way; a seamless horizon with some legion approaching, roaming into far sands. This exalted army fated to vanish into a mirage by their unknown fading charade. My end was to rise again, to see more prosperous years counting within. To envision better and new rejuvenated wistful and olden dreamy days. In this body, a sacrifice – the kingdom of our souls with honor, strength, and grace we've praised.

All that you see here, take it in with every breath, for one day it shall all be gone. Until then, I shall stalk amongst the sands, plaguing with every step, to all who are unlucky to have crossed my path.

And when the dark day does beckon in shades of gray, black, and ash... The Ysombrel, the outlaster and vanquisher, awaits. As I stand upon piles of their remains, defying this deathly necromancer has put them in their place.

And when it ends, all ties severed and gone, the cold grave awaits like so many before. A final departure, wraith-like in form, into darkness forever I go...

-Vhelsraek Ysombrel, the wicked vampire of the north.

A Darkness pervades the mind of this ship.

Apart of this void, a fated whim; a shadowy reminder of old centuries of the past, all now a part of a bygone emperor's crypt...

In the endless time of a vast empty space, it fills this mind with vengeance and entropic hate.

The enemy lies in the invisible winds, star-drift across treacherous space - their time finite, a shadow riddled toll to be paid.

Take these things, these deserved dwellings of doom, now your banished destiny... not a fate given to false portent.

Once more, the empire of the begotten will reign omnipotent again.

-writings of the necro-cryonic vampire,

Xildrakvor Malkhaphros

A long forgotten ghost, a haunted soul he roams, still as bare as the bleached bones, that scattered across the necropolis, amongst them he still does walk.

Faded battles of jousts supreme around empty graves, for as a man he would never kill his prey.

Only to the dawn did he befall shadows, and in his wake he fell many foes before his dying day.

The messages fall upon blind eyes who care not to see or save.

Messages adrift like the wind, those now mourned days.

Atop the summit of the divide's peak I can see far from here, but the snow hides all I seek.

Even she, that one in disguise, met in the snow and fought a final time.

But this drifting wind can only travel to a heart that beats the same only so far.

Now just wind, memory, and dust.

Dying words fading in our time as a monolith to the old monk Zennael Ryjitsu, holding a place among the dead warriors of the ancients, now by spirit, in that ghostly form he roams.

But with a heavy heart he will spend eternity in this dying land.

A place of unfed dreams, a stifled humanity now unveiled before hope, and with a sacred rhythm, breathes.

After so many times in so many fights in the voidance whirlwind that is that realm.

I am taken aback at the memory in ghost form, a mind with no voice haunting the bleached bones of the necropolis I roam.

With a thought of the girl, her soul far now; somewhere on the cliffs of a divide I know not of, a forgotten time of time long ago.

So I wait, and keep time in spirit, that one day I could know if a dragon's heart seeks past death to find its love.

How time passes in my fading time among these old bones I haunt still.

-Zennael Ryjitsu, the mad monk of Freeport.

Love...couldn't be spoken more true, the one who has fought the monk's fight. I've found the dream I've suffered for in time, my sweetest Habibti, her soul together with mine, not even death parts the long awaited dream in life, a love to find, the greatest love this life has known, none so much as this star has shone. A monk then, a warlord after gone, an old hermit ronin who remembered his many comrades, back to back fighting wars. A peace to find, I've sought these dreams for so long and now as real with black wings we fly. When I'm done creating my drawings of her, poems, the heart of the Djinni, and lyric, her tears shed, I embrace, hold, and comfort her spirit. A gallery by the sea, devoted to his dear Habibti will be. Time is not limitless, this is what life was meant for, bō stick sheathed. Every piece will be placed, our tomb will be there. A thousand years, the Taj was built on riches and jewels in stone, but our temple will be crafted out of pure creativity and more, the inspiration of love. Never have I met a soul such as this, rare, unique, dark sensual treasures of the deep. Pure, as mountain water, from snow to snow, the purest, clearest love this life has known, perhaps many hundreds of lives more. My Habibti, the deepest love impassioned and now a living dream, awake, take us by her carved coral mermaid. A love so sweet, everything done with purest love, this sweet, precious princess I long to hold. If I knew she would be, years ago I would have suffered as much and more. God brings people together, my mentor would be proud. She's gotta bring out the best in you, the wise, strong man said when he lived, aloud. I stand atop a high peak in mortal flesh now, in the happiest of love, though now just dust, memory, a ghost from the past, among the majestic bones, in the sacred place of their final home, from the Dragon Necropolis, Zennael Ryjitsu looks on.

-Zennael Ryjitsu, the mad monk of Freeport.

The Eternal Heart of the Djinni

Treasures, jewels, ancient ruins filled with gold, these were the things I wandered for in this world alone. I sought love, but always remained without. I was just a poor adventurer for the king, things of spirit and soul would hold my grip only for so long, and yearned for a beauty in these deserts and jungles of years past, where I ceaselessly sought to quell my saddened heart.

The seaside brought me solace in times of grief, where I searched for my mysterious and evasive quarry down this shell ridden beach. A strange but wonderful lamp made of golden brass, drifted at the bottom of one of the tidepools where I hunted in the past. I reached down deep, and pulled up this golden mystery; it was very light, light enough to float amongst the seaweed, and in the sun it gleamed.

At the local town, an oasis of merchants, royalty, and dreams. I took the lamp to the bazaar, the merchants knew nothing of its origin, yet with its ancient luster it shined to me to be more than what it seemed.

That night, the stars that spread out that splashed the dark sky, glinted a feeling of hope, down this alley where I rested with my lamp, behind a palace, royalty I knew nothing of. I felt a wind drift by, as the lamp began to move in my hands, I heard the whisper of an ancient, alluring song. More beautiful than any siren at sea, singing sailors to their doom. A strong wind whirled within the lamp, and out materialized a body, and face. It was ghostly at first, and then more real every second the lamp rocked in my hands.

"That tyrannical king, banished me to this lamp. One of his court witches cast his spell, and now I am trapped forever here inside this empty dream. My name is Jenna, a Djinni, now just one of the jinn."

"You are a beautiful Djinni", I said quietly to the phantasmic creature, a young, gorgeous woman whose fate was cast out to drift forever at sea.

"What can I do for you? Your words strike my soul, what demon would trap you in such a place, the bottom of that dreadful world, where you have been".

"The Sultan guards a secret, that no one knows save for his cohort, the devious princess Shalrehea. That castle holds wickedness, the Sultan guards it from ever being seen. I tried to save the others, I too was once royalty. But he has done away with them, far worse fates than me."

"I am but a dandelion broken, drifting on the wind as I always have been. I could not get the attention of the king, but lucky I am to have found you, to save you from your many accursed years adrift at sea. Is there a curse that binds you where you now exist?

"My heart was calling for a man like you, a man not afraid to stand by what he believes. You would save this whole kingdom if the Sultan was cast down from where he oversees."

"What is it like in your windy dream, in the lamp and so much more, that fate brings to me?"

She stared into my eyes, her dark sensuous eyes, and held my hand. We vanished together into the breeze, to her void, a place where she cried for love to make her free, as much as all that time I wandered like a mirage in the world, a place where this creature longed and breathed. Her real form was more beauteous than the apparition in the air that appeared before me. A beautiful siren, silken black hair that curved around her sweet face, adorned by onyx eyes that gazed into mine. A dark beauty that drifted in this endless abyss, forever beautiful here, a curse that came with the Sultan's wish.

Her breasts were large handfuls of delightful fruits that at the summit of each, were crowned by amazing nipples that to none of the sea could compare for all time, a wonderous set of areolae encircling her jutting nipples so divine. We drifted together in her place of exile, nearly making love, but she kissed with such tenacity, her full soft lips. I could not help but feel every part of her gentle and womanly form with a zeal and ardent whim. She caressed me as I did her, and I made a promise to free her from her place so alone, to make her real in the world where we both could roam.

"You must break the curse by taking the amulet that the twisted Shalrehea wears upon her neck, and bring it to the fountain of wishes as the crescent moon shines in the night so black."

"She stole my beauty, the Sultan had it ordained, she is but a very old witch who conjures beasts from another plane. He fights his wars with them, thus they rule from their throne in lavish life, untouched by the kingdoms troubles, the people's strife.

The Sultan's true form is a horrible viper, he mercilessly caused much bloodshed in his reign for decades in his sinister fights.

"I'll go to the palace at dawn. I'll reveal their true form and rescue you from their evil done. You are such a beautiful lady, even in ethereal form, I could only hope to make you my own."

I traveled into the lush palace disguised as one of the Sultan's royal guards. I saluted every passing general about to harness Shalrehea's monsters, all they lived for was blood and the sword.

I whispered into the lamp, "Soon you'll be free, maybe we can be together once your curse has passed. I'll show you lands I once knew, and though you'll age once more from where you've been sent, your beauty and sweetness can be seen for all to take in, to be alive again. You are the magic that lies within, a fair and beauteous girl, from the ethereal world far beyond the waves, deep in abyss beyond. My days have been treacherous, there is no rest, no love to find in this life, it is my greatest test. To wander alone is my curse, seemingly my life's ill-fated quest."

I silently approached the final door, where beyond lay the Sultan and Queen fast asleep. I stole into the room and plucked the amulet from the sinister Shalrehea, not waking either snake nor witch.

The guards caught me after taking the trinket kept to seal my dear djinni away. They took my precious lamp, but I hid the amulet in the fountain of wishes this day before being taken to my cage.

The moon changed many more times, from waning gibbous to half moon, as I was kept deep in the palace's dark dungeon alone. The lamp was out of my hands, I could not rescue Jenna to give her back her rightful place on the throne. I fought beasts in the pits below, winning many duels put on for a show, with makeshift weapons, a gladiator doomed to fight there forever on.

The moon was to shine a crescent this night, and my promise to the beautiful djinni trapped against her will must be fulfilled. I prayed that I might escape, and heard in the darkness a whisper, of dead magi of past fates, perhaps a spell of sorts to free me from my own ill-fated end. "Al Jabari lock-em-up, free her again" the dungeon echoed with whispers. What kind of sorcery is this I wondered, and the heavy door slid open, now to find where the lamp was kept.

The palace was silent and empty, and there lay upon a sacrificial altar, my dear djinni. I embraced her, and for many years to come, called that palace home. We abolished the malevolence that plagued it within, and made it beautiful for all.

One day my habibti's loving kiss slowly began to harden me, I could not move. The witch and snake didn't dare to return, but their curse was so strong, that all her years within the lamp made me into a statue, as the Sultan's viper slid up my arm.

Then the beautiful djinni said, "This whole land was being held against its will for so long, I didn't know you'd become stone and leave me once I was free to roam". Shalrehea's image, showing her true form, crowed and clawed at the djinni now many years a mortal. Old and decrepit, she crawled away, being banished by the reappearing minions used to hold the empire in her sway.

Though undeserved, forever I become, a part of the throne, turned to solid stone. I could still hear Jenna's beautiful voice chant that ancient song. So, she searched scrolls over, spoke to wise men near and far, how my petrified body could have fluidity once more.

The day came when she was very old with no cure, and had placed my visage in the gardens among flowers and thorns, of an adventurer she once had known. So she wrapped her hands around his, closed her eyes, and after not long, the sun sank into the sands of this magical oasis, her beauty returned, she too became stone. The night's stars remembered a time when both majestic statues lived, the adventurer from faraway lands, and the beautiful djinni, forever beautiful once more. Forever they stood, through storm and rain, many empires razed and built, together, they both heard the whispers of their ancient song go on.

A plaque mysteriously left by their forms forever frozen in time in that palace garden read:

Treasures, jewels, ancient ruins filled with gold, these were the things I wandered for in this world alone. The real gems of this life are not out there in the caves of the past, but in the hearts of two souls who found each other, who sought love, and finally forever it had come.

* Camera tilts up to the darkened night sky full of stars over the palace roof, scene closes *

The Empty Heart in the Cold Snow   12/27/10

Sometimes within the cold shadow of myself, in the unknown
dream called the girl, I wander the frozen shores of this drifting
world, its pale and empty barren space. A void of treacherous
snowdrift, anticlimactic frost unto a realm far too often I find
myself lost in - this chilling and below zero place. In this life I
remain an abominable spectre in the caves of my past; a shivering
spectacle shaded over by no dreams of love ever had. Endothermic
in their cold nature, their oblivious spirits pass my long desolate
years and fruitless trials by. Now frost stricken branches, these
bones age older, with skin getting colder, melting slowly as I am
forced to walk and tumble into empty wastes. It is a curse to keep,
to wander this earth without. Eternally encased in a frozen shell,
this body, an icy prison entombed like a forsaken revenant, I cast
that cold shadow now no matter where I roam. For the only one
who would ever bear any warmth is by a far-fetched encounter
amongst the tundra of a chilling wind-swept Antarctica. She would
only hold me there alone, and then this unknown dream called the
girl would only do so, to avoid the cold.

For Lisa: A Eulogy   12/5/10

A calm, kind lady from far-away isles, her life in peaceful
demeanor; an interesting and patient, willful way – always giving,
seeing past anything to grant the wish and forget what could
represent pain. A gentle and respected mother, in the company of
those that did keep a smile shining through a once young girl's
beauty. An endless love through the years in her time; a strong
stature in any strife, as kind words through her always soothing
inside, keeping us hopeful in life. And though she has gone into
where we want it to be peaceful and safe, her comforting, giving
soul, who watches from afar, now rests in our inevitable sleep…
with her a timeless prayer, though her visage unto us will no longer
grace, may Lisa be in total peace as she always was in her kind
ways.

There was an island I once knew, a yearning land distant from me, drifting somewhere I first saw it as a mirage of an aura of rapacious energy, harmonized with crashing waves of life's vast seas. Riding this wrecked raft, trembled and ruined by years upon the ocean, landing in a fog ridden night on unknown shores that saved this lost and empty voyage. This makeshift vessel falling apart along the fair shores of this unknown, yet blessed sight. On the new day, a sun paints the only gold here I seek, as birds free in their whim fly amongst a canopy of palms holding fruit I cannot reach.

The ones in the distance who roam in the tribe afar came here long ago, though I thought this isle was unsettled, as ghostlike as all that time on that raft I named Banshee, I wailed upon never-ending relentless waves. The youth wanted trinkets, I gave them old keys with a metal heart in chains, that kept me comforted on the nights where my raft could have sank. The elders wanted to know why to their island I came, asking from what direction the wind pulled me to safety, but I told them by tides I could not leave. Long years kept me from recalling where I hailed, so with the tribesman and tribeswoman we had a feast.

"Our only noble daughter at the edge of the lava is the new sacrifice; it's not our wish she dies. There is a dire fiend that stalks this island, killing all of our people, a walking serpent wanting only to steal life. She was put there, her blood to appease this beast as a final sacrifice. Beyond the messenger's wishes we secretly made a pitfall near her full of spikes."

I thought of this gorgeous land, a place of infinite beauty, though my stay was short, of rivers and dignified fields, an unravaged picture of precious green untouched by man elsewhere and his strife. A cloaked shadow stepped off into the distance behind a tree, an ominous presence of eyes.

"Why must this creature feed on those here? What can I do to stop this evil from its senseless plight?" "There are few men here, and none brave enough to save our last line of blood, our poor daughter's life." "I'll stop it and rescue her, it's the least I can do for this sacred place." "The Leviathan awaits then, let us say a prayer she is safe."

The moon was full this night, and as I went weaponless far through a swampy hill, there she was high up near lava flow, hoisted on stakes by a grim idol of the tribe's sullen, yet necessary representation of protective spirit. The serpent clawed through the foliage, trailing me here this whole time passed, and as it slashed through the breeze, it slithered into the pitfall trap. Her ropes came free, and without knowing each other's form of communication, we embraced as the rain on the temple grounds tapped. Our understanding went beyond mere words, for I had saved the island home of the innocent villagers, keeping their only kin safe. We talked in misshapen words, signs, and eye contact. She knew what I meant, and we knew how we felt. A drifting breeze gave memory on the way back days later atop a peak about lands I once knew; they were no longer home, an empty past. This island with its wonders would turn into a soon sad forgotten love. We both hid beneath jungle cover, and a forbidden, yet sacred act was done. The night could have been forever, fading into long years at sea; a time more full in this one night than all that time out there in pitch black waters I drifted on.

But the serpent still lived as we travelled to her home. It yearned to live to consume all. As we side by side walked as one, our hands locked, some love after all the years at sea I longed, the dreaded evil making noises in the brush on its last haunt, raised its head and flung a poisoned dart. Seeing this wretched thing bring its last energy to bear, I stepped in front of this girl, a love I barely knew, a final road at least now with some direction, I took the envenomed spike through the heart, a silent affection. She leapt up to the branches above, pushing the creature off to its last doom. She rushed beside me, embraced with a kiss, and cold by the serpent's slimy touch. "Don't die and leave me alone." "This island and its mysteries are pure magic, a longing dream. My journey was worth all efforts to save you and find a moment in life where upon a gleam of love, had some meaning." The sun sank down into the ground, planting a tear for the mysterious voyager, from where he came they did not know, his eyes now closed. A somber tale they still tell on this island to the young, about a man who had nothing left to lose, to save their only princess, he died to keep her well. This island's special girl named Catalina.

Within this void of empty space in time now passed by with age fading my life away, unable to partake in every other man's known task. Flesh cold to me; an empty life of blood without being. To stalk the earth without any prey in a meaningless cyclone turned to a somber hate. Years keep a constant life limited, while fate plans to contrive a yearnful ending. The stump knows not even its own grace it held by ages in its beauty; now time gone in its own unknown winds that rip roots out in the grounded fog that lurks, lacking any more reason. Unable to rise above the shade that covers its death, this wooden family guards its ancestor's place of rest. A time in me I no longer can find amongst feminine beauty and ways despised, keeping no hope in love anymore in friendly, yet universally sullen eyes. Shadows escaping each other's shade we both walk alone by, though our trees now grasp the cold earth, and fading intents on inevitably fruitless paths in black winds that flow up as emptiness of hollow heights that make time for another, as others steal our power because they think they are forgiven in life. This stump makes hollow time seem too long; my flesh cannot endeavor to be anything to anyone when it never was. The world is too vast and cold now in shiver, with no shelter but this tree in its youth, and my fading time unable to create in three decades a spring's season of us together. Should my life be cut compared to the rest of others' perception of time's basis as the only flow to nature, then even unloved all through this empty space and void, this flesh I shed and soul to tether, let it be severed, and never to return as abandoned on this anathema of lonely branches with only a vanishing shadow to walk alone forever. Shadows looking back as this old stump's hollow need not remember.

All the time finding an end. Now time with life, every second tiring of instinct and faith.

Entombed at all times, if not in the cold ground, but within, perhaps we feel to pass on, we end the same way.

No reason to go on... to end it whilst all manner of life is seen. Millions of forms - apparitions walking asleep by an endless dream. Living, while dying, as emptiness entraps each of us - our purpose, still unseen.

Looking out amongst the snow ridden plains, reflecting barren fields within. Knowing well a peace all the world keeps. Yet we, somber, with doubtful faith, gaze upon earth's youth eternal carved to its face. Counted time foretelling our own deathly untold age. Improving this thing inevitably locked to fate – the soul unattached; a key by which this mortal shell is cracked by lack of sense, insanity, for many, bitter rage.

It will not change, this vision I weep. For centuries in time tiring of long numbered years, slowly slipping away; as imprints of self undermine power, to make others less inferior. Unto a higher being our lives we stake; truly, the hollow past brings the only wraiths.

To amuse the soul is what remains, as love never existed five and two decades. Caged inside a psyche not letting go, with its dusty, cold grip it glows. Begin to finish what afflicts life... for we are all here only to create - through it, strife.

So, the dark swath of time's end means only yet another death, dying several times in life again to finally ascend. In the children the song goes on; nadir to the zenith from youth born. Yet as I bleakly stare at the melting white distance, instinct becomes lust; love, faith. A life lived dead, absence of amorous gain. In flesh and thought alone, alone in an empty dream, as all eternity awaits erased, perished... unloved in the grave.

Lyrics for my song, Mission San Miguel   8/7/07

San Miguel... Out in the desert you buried them so well.
Holy requisition before the cross, a holy chapel I knelt before god.
In my soul I weep, I held that place within. Hone innocent time;
infinite rhythms of eternal time, oh yeah...

San Miguel. I bought the cross. San Miguel. I took the seed. San
Miguel. I got the cross. San Miguel, I saw the inhabitants that dwell.

Such monklihood we appreciate, such chaste we contemplate, such
temperance we've never known – ohoooh.

But now I pray for my own future life, and I know that I gotta strife,
cuz the blood within seeks her out. I don't know anymore why I'm
around. Vampir to stay young, so long... stay young and die, just a
flip within like a soul tomb.

I try to sing but it comes out all wrong, and if I went back to San
Miguel, I wonder if I made a wish it would turn out so well.

I wonder why, if I could be holy in time. I wonder if this curse of
vampirism is broken. And now, I have that cross... that Valek knew
he never lost, in the sun I go, into the night I go, I wonder why,
Melissa's soul – ohoooh.

San Miguel calms well. And the inhabitants of that grave, I wonder
why, wonder why, wherever they've gone, all of them why. What
they've known. I say a prayer may their souls rest in time.
Diego... Diego.

Belief merely satisfies inspiration.

Darkness clouds the imagination.

Whispers of heavenly angels sing in evasion.

Silence breaks the noise of unwanted guests,

Thrown out by frustration.

To move one so unmoved, ripples into their skin in aggravation.

I find what love I can in nothing,

And so to that end, it is what I receive.

But in the end, it is merely only simple belief.

Nighttime takes in the moon lacking the man, a distant cousin of her unknown sins... A way to part yet meet, by stars quarreling but distant, a timeless flow of ends we seek.

Happiness is the cradle that rocks us in comfort through life. Love besides emotion never was needed before we were created as infants, against a world outside.

Free the mouse from its cage. It's better to see the creature die to live, than live to die.

Where you roam you hide your face behind a mask well known. It looks like you, since it fits your dangerous ways so well. After your heart bleeds without disdain, we still fight in the darkest rain.

People who cannot be creative can be dangerous people.

Fenced out by love and dreams combined. My will is lost to hope always wrong inside, and so by willing ills, each love in turn becomes blind.

A man's love is easy to judge, but thy lady's wishes are not.

Restrained love damages the Psyche.

The stronger the inspiration, the more powerful the creation.

Death is when our passion dies; to compromise your truth, becoming lies.

What you put your love in you cannot be ashamed to show. Others can see that love and feel love in their hearts as well.

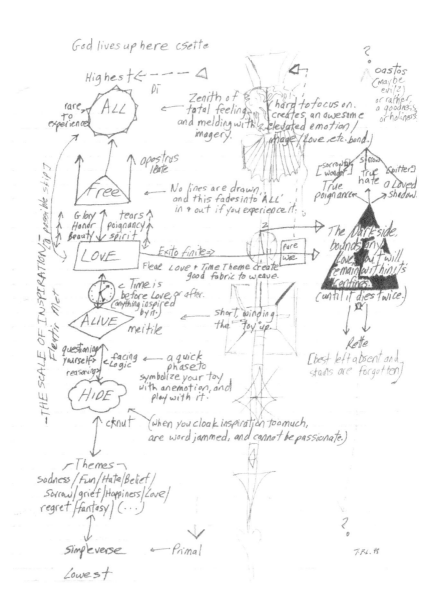

God lives up here csette

Highest ←---- △

DT

Zenith of total feeling and melding with imagery.

rare to experience

ALL

hard to focus on. creates an awesome & elevated emotion/ image (love, etc. bond.)

?
oastos (maybe evil?) or rather a goodness or holiness

Free

opostrus leate

← No lines are drawn, and this fades into 'ALL' in & out if you experience it.

[sorrow/ wonder]   sorrow
True   True   [bitter]
poignance hate a loved
                  shadow.

Glory Honor Beauty   tears poignancy spirit

LOVE

← Exito finite ⇒

Please Love + Time Theme create good fabric to weave.

pure we

The Dark side, bound in your Love, you will remain within its confines.

(until it dies twice.)

← Time is before Love, or after. (anything inspired by it.)

ALIVE   meitile

← Short, winding the "toy" up.

Rette
[best left absent and stains are forgotten]

questioning yourself → facing reasoning → Logic

← a quick phase to symbolize your toy with an emotion, and play with it.

HIDE

↑ cknut (when you cloak inspiration too much, are word jammed, and cannot be passionate.)

⌐ Themes ¬
sadness / Fun / Hate / Belief /
Sorrow / grief / Happiness / Love /
regret / fantasy / (...)

simple verse   ← Primal

Lowest

—THE SCALE OF INSPIRATION (a possible skip)—
Fleetir Met

?

T.F.G. 45

Interacting with so many rhymed sounds, through introspection I deciphered the alphabet somewhat.

A - Manly Objective.

B - Objective - (Ball, boy, bad, bite).

C - Self Induced.

D - A sacrificing yet very true, firm sound. Encompassing in some instances.

E - Truthful sound, feministic, sensory, or liking.

F - Self Surfacing.

G - Egoistic sound, also a transparency of itself or self reflecting.

H - A gathering of self.

I - Only to one, no more.

J - Fun, jazzy.

K - Purposive sound - (Key, kill, kind, keep, or morphing a name like Crystal to Krystal).

L - The lying sound, or sincerely truthful!

M - A bad sound, desireful sound, or soothing unto the self.

N - A forgetting sound. Protects sacredness.

O - Awe.

P - A very picturing sound.

Q - Tricky.

R - Preceding an all-inclusive, and after.

S - Truth in a minimal sense - strange in a person using it too much.

T - Trying.

U - An opposite indirection.

V - A sound imposing harsh, strong, or vehement words.

W - Questioning.

X - Known, yet unknowing.

Y - Ponderance.

Z - Known, yet mysterious.

If you can cry over anything non-sexual, non-affectionate, or loving, then it can become a vice. Any kind of vice – to drink anything making you drunk, too much sleep, too much food, too much anything, could be a vice - at least not consciously. To cry inside over a thing loved enchantedly, eternally, longingly sentimental, - not just crying, but all its forms; longing, love not able to be freed to join love that does, but does not exist, and love that bonds and searches to, but failingly does, is the magic of my poetry.

Made in the USA
Middletown, DE
05 March 2023

26169804R00099